The Most Wealth for the Least Work Through Cooperation

By

Bob Blain, Ph.D.

Emeritus Professor of Sociology
Southern Illinois University Edwardsville

First published by AuthorHouse 04/15/04

ISBN: 1-4140-3519-5 (e-book)
ISBN: 1-4184-3872-3 (Paperback)

Library of Congress Control Number: 2004090432

This book is printed on acid free paper.

Printed in the United States of America
Bloomington, IN

The cover photo of a community barn raising is used by permission of the Timber Framers Guild, P.O. Box 60, Becket, MA 01223. Website: http://www.tfguild.org.

In July 2000, members of the Timber Framers Guild joined with guests of Gould Farm and volunteers from across the country in rural, southwestern Massachusetts to cut the timbers for a big barn and then raise the barn in a daylong community barn raising. This photo shows some of the many volunteers who helped raise the barn that day in July. On one of the barn's timbers is carved Gould Farm's motto: "We harvest hope."

The Timber Framers Guild is a non-profit educational association that hosts conferences, supports research, and offers a series of hands-on workshops, along with opportunities for community service building projects. The barn is an example of one such project developed by the Guild to educate members and the public in the theories and techniques of timber framing.

Gould Farm is the oldest therapeutic community in the nation for adults with mental illnesses, including schizophrenia, bi-polar disorder, and severe depression. Gould Farm is based on the belief that work is healing.

Dedicated to

Benjamin Bellamy Blain
June 9, 1981 - October 16, 1999

Named in honor of Edward Bellamy (1850-1898) whose utopian novel, *Looking Backward: 1887-2000,* inspired millions to believe that the most wealth with the least work could be achieved. Although an automobile accident kept Ben from reaching 2000, as his dad I am proud to carry on the quest in his memory.

And to
Brian Buckminster Blain, 16

Named in honor of Richard Buckminster Fuller (1895-1983), who promoted the wisdom of doing more with less. May Brian grow in wisdom as he grows in age.

Table of Contents

Acknowledgements

My thanks to J. W. Smith for his great book on *The World's Wasted Wealth* that alerted me to the many ways we can increase our real wealth while reducing work time and for encouraging me to publish my own work. Thanks also to Ken Bohnsack for his successful efforts to obtain support from nearly 4,000 tax-supported bodies in the U.S. for his proposal to have Congress make available money for public goods interest free. I encourage interested readers to contact them through the Internet at:

The Institute for Economic Democracy

http://www.ied.info

Ken Bohnsack

kbohnsack@insightbb.com

The ideas in this book are based on more than 35 years of research and teaching as a university professor and are supported by the rigorous challenge of simulation with Cooperation: The Wealth of Nations Game. You can download the simulation free from:

The Hour Money Institute for Global Harmony

http://hourmoney.org

My thanks also to Bob Gill, co-inventor of the Cooperation: The Wealth of Nations Game who also designed the cover and did several of the drawings in this book.

I also thank my wife, Mary, for understanding my need to publish these ideas.

Chapter 1

The Most Wealth for the Least Work

Work smarter, not harder. Network with others. Cooperate. Everything is easier when everybody helps. Build quality, not quantity. Achieve development, not growth. Do more with less. Conserve. Save time. Save money. Make the rules of the game so that everyone wins.

What's in it for you? The answer includes economic well-being and security, more free time to enjoy life, more generally, a world at peace, and people prospering everywhere.

You are already way ahead of the game. You were born *HUMAN*. What a wonderful advantage and opportunity you have. You stand on two legs, allowing you to move across the earth. Your arms and hands are free. Your opposable thumbs empower you to grasp objects. Your mouth, lips, teeth, soft palate, and larynx give you the power to make hundreds of voice sounds. Your ears, nose, eyes, and skin bring multidimensional information from all around you. On top of it all is your brain, beyond comprehension in thinking power and storage capacity.

Sure, when we get the rules right, there will still be some illness, waste, foolishness, and sorrow, but much less than now. Think of life as a continuum, a scale from the worst of times to the best of times.

Worst of times   X   Best of times.

I've put the X where I think life is for more than half of the six billion people on earth today. The United Nations estimates that as many as two billion people live in abject poverty, without clean water to drink, no place to properly dispose of human waste, hungry most of the time, slum housing or worse. It's terrible.

1

Others live better than Pharaohs and kings of old. Their X would be at the top of the scale, Best of times, except for all the misery they have to hear about and fear.

Why can we have well-being, security, and free time worldwide? Mother Earth has more than enough for everyone. The energy that reaches the earth from the sun in four days is more than all the energy stored in all the coal, oil, and natural gas on earth.

Do you think the problem is too many people on earth?

Think about this. If everyone on earth were six feet tall, a foot and a half wide, and a foot thick, we could all fit in a box that would measure less than three quarters of a mile on each side. Here's the math if you doubt it. A person six feet tall, a foot and a half wide, and a foot thick would occupy nine cubic feet. In round numbers:

A 5280' by 5280' by 5280' cube: 147 billion cubic feet.

Number of people alive today: 6.3 billion.

Nine cubic feet multiplied by 6.3 billion people: 57 billion cubic feet.

Cubic feet in a three quarter mile cube: 62 billion.

Number of people that would fit in a mile cube: 16 billion.

In short, a human population almost three times larger than it is today would fit in a box that measured one mile on each side.

We could not live in such a box. That's not my point. My point is that Mother Earth is a lot larger and we are a lot smaller than we might think. There is plenty of room on earth for all of us. Consider also that every time we build a building with more than one floor in it, we add to the "land" area of the earth. The sun and earth together provide everything we need.

So what's wrong? Why are we bombarded every day with all that bad news?

Believe it or not, the root cause is simple. I don't mean easy to grasp, nor do I mean easy to correct. I mean simple. Recently, we had a new engine put in our 1984 Volkswagen van. It ran terribly. It would idle fine, but at low speeds, it jerked and choked. It seemed that we had wasted our money on that new engine. We wondered: Was it time to trash the old thing? I took it to an old timer who has repaired Volkswagens for more than 30 years. I watched him look it over. He found a few unrelated problems: two wires unplugged, one broken, and a missing hose clamp. With those fixed, the engine still ran terribly, surging and idling, surging and idling. Then he noticed a wire across a flap of metal that prevented it from moving. He pushed the wire out of the way and the engine has run fine ever since. I had to look up what the flap of metal was. It was the throttle valve.

That problem was simple and easy to fix. The problem preventing us here and everywhere worldwide from having the kind of life we all deserve and that the earth makes possible is nearly as simple. It is that the monies of the world have no unit defining their value. We are all left guesstimating the value of money. We guess the value of our own money reasonably well because we use it every day, but the value of foreign currencies for most people is as unintelligible as the foreign languages spoken in those countries. Contrast that situation with the length of a meter. No matter what language is spoken in a country, the length of a meter is the same everywhere. We need a unit for money with the same certainty, stability, and fairness (accuracy) as the length of a meter.

You might hear people say that finding such a unit is impossible. If we believed that new ideas were impossible, there would be no telephones, televisions, or airplanes. Not only is a universal unit for money possible, it already underlies 90 percent of the present exchange rate values of the monies of the world. That unit is an hour of work. We will get the most wealth for the least work by adjusting all monies to an hour of

3

work. This simple change, simple because it is a matter of simple arithmetic, will make cooperation easier and fairer everywhere. But I am getting ahead of my story. Let me set the moral context for this simple monetary change with the words of Kahlil Gibran in *The Prophet* (1923).

The earth yields her fruit,

If you but know how to fill your hands.

It is in exchanging the fruits of the earth

That you shall find abundance and be satisfied.

But unless the exchange be in love and kindly justice,

It will but lead some to greed and others to hunger.

Our destiny as human beings is to have the most wealth for the least work. All of human cultural development is aimed at that goal. Mother Earth is too rich in resources and the sun is too generous with energy for us not to live with the most wealth for the least work. There have been many delays and detours along the way; many obstacles and myths have led us astray. You may have heard it said that "greed is good." I don't think so. Greed is so bad that it is a cardinal sin in Catholicism. Greed is viewed as good through the eyes of supply and demand competitive economics, which was built on the sandy foundation of money as we know it today. Money is doing a poor job of encouraging everyone to share the work and share the wealth. Instead, money in its present primitive form allows people to hoard money or work or both.

When you first read the title of this book, did you think it might be about making a lot of money without doing any work? There are many schemes around for making money. Test such schemes by asking if they benefit everyone or if one party is shifting the burden of his support onto the shoulders of others. Is it a way for one person to get the wealth while the other person gets the work?

The lottery is one of those "I win you lose" schemes. Millions of people buy tickets, hoping to be the Big Winner. Jackpots are millions of dollars. What does it take for one person to be the Big Winner? Millions of people must lose. It's a zero-sum game; one person wins and another person loses (+1 -1= 0). In this book, my goal is to explain how we can get the most wealth for the least work through cooperation. We need to make life a plus-sum game. If I win, then you win (+1+1=2). We win together.

Let me be clear about how I define wealth. I mean having what is necessary to be healthy and happy, which includes good food, clothing, housing, friendly neighbors, easy access to education and travel, a satisfying occupation, and plenty of free time to enjoy life.

By wealth I don't mean lots of money. That definition of wealth confuses extravagance and waste with health and happiness. Human needs and wants are not much different from one person to another. The details vary but the basics are the same. A person can only consume so much food, wear so much clothing, live in so much housing, and occupy so much space at one time. We are born the same way, require the same care and support growing up, face similar challenges in our adult lives, and eventually face death.

When I use the word "wealth," I will always mean well-being. Notice that wealth and health differ only by one letter. A healthy person is, by that fact alone, wealthy. A happy person is that much wealthier. A wise person is perhaps the wealthiest of all. With that meaning of wealth clearly in mind, let us examine the myth that the most wealth with the least work can be achieved by having some people receive all the wealth while other people do all the work.

Some people receiving all the wealth while other people do all the work is wrong on both counts. It produces neither the most wealth nor the least work. Ask yourself how much wealth the recipients produce when they do not do any work. They will produce no wealth. So the total wealth produced will be reduced by the amount they would have produced.

Now consider the people who do all the work but receive little or no wealth. Will they work to their fullest ability? Probably not. They are more likely to feel resentment and anger, feelings that will reduce their productivity. Therefore, it is easy to see that when some people are wealthy without working and others work without becoming wealthy, we cannot achieve the most wealth with the least work.

In my opinion, the way to achieve the most wealth with the least work is for everyone to *share the work and share the wealth*. Consider how that might work. With everyone doing a share of the work, everyone would be producing a share of the wealth. The wealth produced by person A would add to the wealth produced by person B, which would add to the wealth produced by person C and so forth. Wealth would be additive: 1 + 1 + 1 + 1 = 4. Total wealth then would be equal to the total number of people working to produce wealth.

There is something very special about people working together; namely, they can do things together that are impossible to do alone. R. Buckminster "Bucky" Fuller called it *synergy*. With cooperation, wealth can *multiply*. Things can be done that can only be done, or done much better, by people working together. Take the simple example of fishing.

Imagine a lone fisherman waiting patiently for the fish to take the bait. How many fish is that person likely to catch? Not many. Why not? The fish have the whole lake in which to swim. What is the likelihood that they will swim by the one spot where our lone fisherman happens to be? It's slim.

From the National Oceanic & Atmospheric Administration Central Library

Now consider fishing as a team. The team can form a large circle to surround an area, and then move toward each other. This will drive the fish into the center of the circle where the fishermen can scoop them up in a net.

Commercial fishing today is cooperative. Teams of people with boats and large nets scoop hundreds of fish at a time. For example, the fishing industry in Alaska employs over 65,000 people. The state's fisheries average over $11.2 billion in revenue per year and account for nearly 38 percent of the dollar value of fish and seafood landed in the United States.

Many things are like fishing; they are much more productive when done by groups of people. I think of the example of building a barn. A team can easily do what one person alone would probably find impossible. As the Chinese say, "Many hands

make light work." I hope to show in this book that the key to the most wealth with the least work is sharing the work and sharing the wealth. The main obstacle to achieving that goal today is money.

Chapter 2

Time Money: The Currency Evolution

The central problem of our time is money. The lack of money and the uneven distribution of money are but symptoms of the problem in the same way that a fever is a symptom of an underlying disease. It is that money has no observable quantity to define its value. It has no known denominator, only a name without a definition, in the case of the United States, "dollar."

The physical forms of money are not the problem. Quite the contrary, in the ways we produce, handle, and process it, money has reached a pinnacle of technological perfection. The paper money we use is printed from finely engraved plates on high quality paper and our coins are minted from finely engraved molds. In recent years, plastic cards and computers have enabled us to deposit and withdraw money from ATM machines widely available many miles from the banks where we have our accounts. These are truly marvels of modern technology. The problem is not in the physical form of our money. The problem is in the uncertain value of our money. That uncertainty arises from the absence of a definition of the unit of our money.

Every country in the world has its own name for its money. In the United States, we call our money "dollars." Other countries call their money "pesos," "dinars," "yen," "kroners," "rupees," "soles," "drachmas," "won," "kwacha," and many other names. They all share the same defect: the unit to which they refer is undefined. So how does anyone know the value of a peso, a yen, or a kwacha?

We must all judge the value of our money inductively. We see the prices of many things: candy bars, gasoline, rent, cars, clothes, theater tickets, and so forth. From these specific prices we form a general idea of the value of a dollar. Then, as prices change, we change our general sense of the value of a dollar. We proceed from the specific to the general.

We do precisely the opposite with all other forms of measurement. With measures of length, volume, and weight, we proceed deductively. We start with the general standard and apply that standard to each specific case. For example, a yardstick tells us the length of a yard in general. We then use the yardstick to measure the length of a specific piece of cloth, the length of a specific room, or the height of a specific person.

By starting with the standard, we know *exactly* the length of a yard and a meter. We also know, or can easily find out, exactly how to convert yards to meters. A yard is 36 inches. A meter is 39.36960 inches. If anyone has any doubt about the length of a yard or meter, all they need to do is find a yardstick or a meter stick. The physical length of the stick defines the meaning of the words "yard" and "meter."

Because they are based on observable physical quantities, the units of the Metric System are exactly the same everywhere in the world. The result is that people measure length, volume, weight and many other quantities every day easily and routinely without dispute. There are never strikes by people demanding an increase in the length of the meter or the volume of a liter.

The world economy functions smoothly whenever and wherever units of the Metric System are used. We have no market where buyers and sellers haggle over those standards. We have no banks publishing daily quotations of changes in their units. They are stable and certain. Imagine the mess we would have if units of length, volume, and weight were inflating and deflating from one day to the next and from one year to the next. A global economy would be impossible. Nothing could be produced in one country to be assembled in another country because the measurements would not match. Yet we have that situation with money.

There is a currency exchange rate market, the biggest market in the world, where buyers and sellers bid against each other on the basis of expected rises and falls in the values of different monies. We hear from time to time that "the dollar has risen in value relative to the yen" or that "the dollar has weakened relative to the euro." If the altitude and speed of aircraft depended on such gyrations, it would never be safe to fly.

What makes the units of the Metric System work is that they are defined by *objective quantities*: physical amounts that people can see. It is a major point in this book that we need a similar objective quantity for every money system in the world. Today "dollar" means different things to different people. We must each estimate its value by trial and error. The result is an undeterminable amount of error. No one knows the value of a dollar with certainty. If you think you know its value today, wait until tomorrow when it will have changed.

We need a definition of dollar that is as clear, stable, and sensible as our definitions of length, weight, and volume. That definition, as I will explain in this book, is work time. We can save both work time and money by marrying them. Everybody knows they are already engaged. We always see them together. Time and money, they work together. We work time and get paid money. They play together. If you have the money, you can spend the time. We invest in time and in money. We save time and money as well as waste time and money. It's time to marry them so that we can all, as they say, live happily ever after.

Chapter 3

Beyond Repair, Remodel

We had a plumber come to the house the other day to look at a big hole in our bathroom shower wall caused by a water leak. After seeing it he said, "This is beyond repair. You need to remodel." Instead of patching the hole, he recommended that we put in a new shower stall. To save time and money, we must go beyond repair.

We can save time and money in ways that are similar to repairing the hole in the shower wall. They include better time management, car-pooling, clipping coupons, having savings automatically deducted from our paychecks, and investing in stocks and bonds. But these are not enough. They save some time and some money, but the savings may not cover the extra trouble they cause.

Our use of time and money today is like an old car. We can tinker with it, fix a little here and fix a little there, and maybe get a few more miles out of it, but at a certain point it would be wiser to get a new model. Just as the design of cars has improved since the first horseless carriages of a century ago, we need an improved model of money. I will explain throughout this book why I think the new model should be hour money.

The new model requires more than making the money more difficult to counterfeit. It is a quantum leap as fundamental as the change from drawing water from a well with a bucket to drawing it from a kitchen tap.

The new model I support did not originate with me. Back in 1832, some people were using money denominated in hours of work. Today, there are people all over the world using money denominated in hours of work. But these are local affairs that have difficulty extending their transactions beyond their local communities. I am proposing the extension of their insight to all monies in the world.

The adoption of an hour of work as the basic unit for money everywhere in the world can save us large amounts of time: days, weeks, months and years. It can save us *life time*. The new model can reduce the intensity of work, not increase it. It can transform our lives from mostly work to mostly doing things by choice for fulfillment and enjoyment. We can work by choice and have all the money we need. We can do things because we want to do them. Today, in the pursuit of happiness, there is too much pursuit and not enough happiness. With time money, we can have less pursuit and more happiness.

J.W. Smith, in *The World's* Wasted *Wealth 2* (1994), explains the many ways that we waste our lives doing unnecessary work. He lists several serious students of our way of life who have been telling us for the past 100 years that we could be working a fraction of the time we work now and still live at a higher standard than we live today. They have been asking if we have the workweek and the weekend backwards. Could we be working two days a week with five days off? Does it not seem odd that, although we have laborsaving devices and mass production, we continue to work as much as we do? Both time and money seem as scarce as ever. Something is wrong, and we need to find out what it is and fix it.

I do not know what you would do with more free time. Much of that depends on personal values and circumstances. I imagine that many of us would use the first few additional hours of free time to do those necessary chores we keep postponing: laundry, housecleaning, car maintenance. With more free time we would probably want to relax, visit our friends and family, and take meals at a leisurely pace. You can add to the list, I am sure.

I suggest that we remodel in a series of steps from the hectic, shortsighted, wasteful non-economy of today to a more leisurely, enjoyable lifetime model. A strategy I propose here is that we reduce the workweek each year by the rate of unemployment. If unemployment is five percent, then we reduce the workweek five percent. This would give working people more free time, shift the unemployed from welfare to work-fair, and reduce taxes.

I am also going to propose a way for prices to go *down* as a general rule rather than up. With prices generally decreasing, the purchasing power of our money will increase as time passes. The money put into a savings account today would gain purchasing power the longer we left it in the bank. We would find ourselves working less time while being paid money that buys more the longer we save it.

The changes I propose are more than repairs but less than revolution. I have already mentioned one change, namely, reducing the time we work by the rate of unemployment. The idea is to proceed by gradual steps, like an architect might plan a new house so that contractors can build it step by step. The result will still look like a house with many familiar features. It will have new features, however, that will make our lives easier, more secure, and more fun.

Chapter 4

The Problem is Entropy, not Scarcity

A new house must start with a level foundation. The economic house we live in today has a foundation that is askew. Like a lens slightly out of focus, economics as we know it today has us slightly out of focus in thinking that the central economic problem is scarcity.

Consult any standard economics textbook and you will find it stating, if not on the first page soon thereafter, that human needs and wants are infinite and there is not and can never be enough goods and services to satisfy those needs and wants. It follows from this assumption that people must compete to decide who will have and who will not have the scarce resources available. In short, scarcity and competition go together. From scarcity follows the need for competition. Let me explain how we need to re-focus.

The problem, as I see it, is entropy, not scarcity. Entropy is the tendency for everything to decay and disintegrate. Entropy is expressed in the Second Law of Thermodynamics as the principle that energy always travels from a warmer location to a cooler location. Energy cannot travel from a cooler to a warmer location. The flow of energy, in that sense, is always downhill. It is this transfer that makes work possible.

Entropy is a measure of unavailable energy. Energy from the sun is the source of most available energy on earth. Plants absorb the sun's energy in the process of photosynthesis; this energy then becomes available to us in the form of food and wood. We eat the food, which fuels our bodies. As our bodies use that energy, available energy is transformed once again into unavailable energy. When we burn the wood, the energy stored in the wood is released, which reverts to unavailable energy.

17

When we cut down trees, saw them into boards, and build structures, we use up available energy in our bodies and in the fuel we use to operate the cutting, transporting, and constructing machines. We gain the use of the structures. They embody available energy as long as we maintain the structures. Maintenance transforms available energy into unavailable energy. Maintenance, however, generally takes less energy than construction, so we are wise to maintain existing structures rather than allow them to deteriorate.

The shift in focus from scarcity to entropy also shifts the focus from competition to cooperation. Competition consumes energy; cooperation conserves it. Our challenge is to minimize entropy. That means we

Entropy

must also minimize work because work transforms available energy into unavailable energy. Work increases entropy. By cooperating, we can use energy more effectively and efficiently.

You can now see scarcity as a *consequence* of competition, not a cause. If we ignore entropy, if we waste available energy, we get scarcity. If we have scarcity and respond to it by cooperating, we minimize entropy and have our best hope of eliminating scarcity. There is already enough food produced in the world to feed every person a healthy diet. A big part of our problem is that food producers and distributors compete with each other, which drives up the real cost (available energy), both human and non-human, of the goods and services that would make us all truly wealthy.

Like the donkeys in the picture, we need to stop competing against one another. We need to ask ourselves what we can do that will conserve energy while meeting all of our needs. The donkeys figured it out. It's time for us to do the same.

Chapter 5

GDP as Gross Domestic Price

Critical to our success is how we measure success. We must have the goal clearly and correctly in view if we are to reach it. Another of the myths that has delayed our achieving the most wealth with the least work is the myth that success requires constantly increasing our Gross Domestic Product.

Today we use the Gross Domestic Product to measure our economic progress. It is obtained by adding the selling prices of all goods and services produced in a country in a year. For example, if a million cars are produced and their average selling price is $15,000, those cars add 1 million times $15,000, or $15 billion to the year's GDP. Construction of the USS Ronald Reagan nuclear aircraft carrier cost four and one half billion dollars ($4,500,000,000) and millions of man-hours. That added to GDP.

Section of the USS Ronald Reagan under construction.

In terms of GDP, the United States is one of the richest countries in the world. For example, in 2001 the GDP of the United States was $10.2 trillion. Given our population of about 300 million, that GDP was $34,026 per person. In round numbers, that meant $34,000 worth of goods and services was produced for every man, woman, and child in the United States. That is equivalent to $654 per person per week.

However, that GDP is not comprised only of household consumer items like food, clothes, and housing. If everyone took $34,000 and tried to spend it all, they would soon buy everything on sale and still have a lot of money left. Why? One answer is that many products are public goods, such as roads, bridges, schools, parks, fresh water supply systems, and waste water treatment plants. It also includes government expenditures for weapons, such as the USS Ronald Reagan aircraft carrier. The government levies taxes to pay for such public goods and services, some that may, and some that may not, add to our well-being. These expenditures reduce the portion of the $34,000 per capita GDP that can be spent on consumer commodities.

Then there are many private capital goods as well, such as new factories and equipment, train lines and trucks, that are included in total production. Furthermore, production itself causes wear on machinery, so deductions must be made to account for these costs.

There are other reasons that the huge level of production, $34,000 per person in 2001, did not translate directly into increased wealth for everyone. The most obvious reason is that the GDP was not distributed equally to everyone. Some people received many times $34,000 while other people received a small fraction of that amount. GDP per person is an average. If I receive a million dollars and you receive nothing, we each receive $500,000 on average. Relying on averages can distort reality. To properly assess the effect of GDP on national well being, we must include how that GDP is distributed.

But there is another less obvious reason that GDP is not a good index of national well being. Destructive events add to the GDP. Every auto accident adds to the GDP, as does every earthquake, hurricane, and flood because they cause damage that costs millions of hours of labor to repair. For the GDP to measure increases in national well being, we would need to *subtract*, rather than add, these costs and all other costs to replace destroyed goods and lost services. There are also costs to clean up the air and water pollution that mass amounts of production cause.

The point here is that we need to find ways to *reduce* the deductions. For example, we could reduce the production of expensive weapons. We could also invest more in maintaining our public and private capital goods, which might be less than the cost of replacing them. The more we maintain, the less labor we will need to replace capital goods. This would reduce the total size of the GDP while increasing the proportion that could represent new real wealth.

The biggest problem I see with GDP is the emphasis on its growth. Thinking that growth equates to greater well-being, to me, is another one of the misconceptions that interferes with achieving our destiny of the most wealth with the least work. Focusing on growth encourages waste rather than development. We could bring a great boon to the automobile industry by junking our cars after driving them a few thousand miles. A large portion of the US economy is dependent on the sale of new automobiles. That market is now saturated with about 50 cars for every mile of highway in the United States.

While replacing all those cars would spike the GDP, imagine all the material and labor that we would waste and the unnecessary pollution it would cause. And yet, taking good care of our cars with regular maintenance and careful driving "hurts" the auto industry. Unsold cars pile up in dealer showrooms; auto assembly plants slow down or close; and thousands of people are laid off. Soon we hear the people affected demanding more jobs in the automobile industry.

We know that nothing on earth can grow forever, including the GDP. From 1960 to 2001, the Gross Domestic Product of the United States increased from $527 billion to $10.2 trillion.

We were not poor in 1960. Still we produced more every year, producing in 2001 nineteen times more than we produced in 1960. Yard sales have mushroomed around the country, I think because people have more stuff than they know what to do with. Look at all the storage units that have been built so people can put their stuff somewhere. How many of us have many times more of everything than we possibly need?

One of the most bizarre things that have happened in recent memory is the advice that government officials gave us after the three commercial jetliners were crashed into the World Trade Center and the Pentagon. We were told to go shopping! The catastrophe was seen as a danger to our economy because it might slow down consumer spending. We have put ourselves in the position of needing to buy more in order to keep the economy accelerating. Imagine trying to keep an automobile always accelerating. That is in effect what we are trying to do by thinking that good economic health requires an ever-growing GDP.

Some GDP growth was due to inflation. Inflation is another factor that misleads us. While the GDP was exploding upward from 1960 to 2001, average wages increased from $2.09 to $14.33 per hour. For forty years, workers generally saw their wages rising, an appearance of progress. Wages were seven times higher in 2001 than they were in 1960. However, the GDP was nineteen times higher in 2001 than in 1960. Although wages were rising, giving workers the impression that they were getting ahead, their share of the product was falling and they were losing ground. Even worse, this scenario does not consider the waste and environmental damage that the explosion of the GDP caused in that time.

In the same forty years, debt grew twenty-eight times higher! Total public and private debt in the United States in 1960 was $1.037 trillion. This debt included the debts of the federal government, state and local governments, corporations, farmers, mortgages, and consumer credit debts. By 2001, total debt stood at $29.496 trillion. And it continues its upward explosion at this moment.

An economist is likely to tell you that a richer economy can handle a larger debt. Here is a double distortion. First, it assumes that a higher GDP means a richer economy when it could mean a poorer one from production pollution, consumer waste, and depleted resources. Second, it argues that being richer means being deeper in debt! Common sense tells us that richer means paying off debt. Again, we see a misconception that denies us achievement of our destiny of the most wealth for the least work.

After forty years of enormous economic growth, do our inner cities look better than they did in 1960? Are fewer people in prison today than in 1960? Do we feel safer walking the streets at night? Are our schools better? Are our roads and bridges maintained better? At a time in human history when the means for a good life for everyone are more available than ever before, every evening those of us who can stand it suffer through bad news from everywhere: our cities, our country, and the rest of the world.

If we were talking about population growth instead of GDP growth, we would be alarmed. What a wreck the earth would be if the population today were nineteen times larger than in 1960. We realize that population could not double and redouble for long before people would starve for lack of food and many resources would be depleted. In the same way, production cannot grow for long before we pollute all the air and water, overheat the atmosphere, and exhaust all the earth's resources in the process, results we are well along in producing.

After all this production it is fair to ask if we are better off today than we were in 1960. What do we have of lasting value to show for all the energy consumed by all this production? We have created mountains of trash, but where is the treasure? A large proportion of trash in our landfills consists of debris from demolished buildings. Many of those buildings were treasures of architecture and workmanship, and yet we demolished them and their demolition added to the GDP.

Economists recognize that GDP is not a good measure of progress and some have proposed a modified GDP that they call the "Genuine Progress Indicator" or the "Green National Product" (Cobb, 1994). Their "new model" takes into account the distribution of income, environmental damage, the value of housework, resource depletion, and several other things. By their calculations, the growth of real value in the US economy ended in 1973. Since then we have been in a decline, one masked by cheap imports.

This new measure, the Genuine Progress Indicator, has come under fire from other economists who object to the value judgements involved in deciding what to add and what to subtract. These economists argue that the only valid value judgements are those made by consumers when they decide to buy goods and services. Here we get to the heart of the problem, namely, the assumption that price reflects value.

The interpretation that GDP always represents an addition to our national well being is built on the assumption that buyers express how much they value a good or service when they choose to pay the price to buy it. If that assumption is correct, then all purchase decisions reflect value and the sum of those values is the annual addition to national wealth, or GDP.

I think that the value assumption is only partially correct. The correct part is that people would not buy something if it had no value to them. When they buy something, they are using their money to say they value what they are buying. Otherwise they would not buy it. So far, so good.

The incorrect part of the value assumption is that price mirrors value, that price reflects *how much* the buyer values the purchased item. I think it is correct to assume that to buy something the buyer must value it *at least* as much as the cost of paying for it. But to the buyer, price is a cost, not a value. Buyers want the most value for the lowest price. That's why buyers would prefer to shop around! That's why sellers advertise that they can sell at lower prices than their competitors. Using the logic that price equates to value, buyers should be looking to pay more for products and sellers should be advertising how much more expensive their products are!

Recently, water was turned off to homes in our city to allow workers to move a water main that stood in the way of the construction of a new gas station. For that day we were without running water. Suddenly we rediscovered the value of indoor plumbing. If we had not drawn some water into bottles before the water was turned off, we would have had to do without it or go to the grocery store and buy bottled water. While the water was off we could not wash clothes or dishes, take showers, or flush the toilet. For several days after the water was turned back on we had to boil water before drinking it.

Our monthly water bill is about $50. With five people in our household, that's $10 per person or 33 cents per person per day. I can say with confidence that every member of my household would agree that the value of running water in our home is far more than 33 cents a day. I take a shower every morning, and I would be miserable all day without one. We like spaghetti once in a while, which requires water to cook the noodles. Coffee requires water as does soup. If we added up all the benefits of having indoor plumbing, it would come to far more than 33 cents a day. We pay the $50 monthly water bill because the benefits exceed the $50 cost. In fact, the benefits cannot be measured in money.

After a hot shower I feel like a million bucks. Putting on a set of clean clothes is a pleasure. Getting the dishes washed and put away spotless is a priceless relief. Values are too qualitative to be measured by money price. Values are too variable from time to time and from person to person to be measured by price.

My boys played in the mud the other day. It took the hose outside to clean off their shoes and a good shower to get the mud off their legs. Their clothes came clean in the washing machine. The water used cost little compared to the value realized. Value varies with circumstances and with persons, although prices rarely change from one person to another. Have you ever had a cashier at a grocery store change a price after asking you how much you wanted each item in your grocery cart? Anyone would be insulted if that ever happened. Money has the power to express price. It cannot express value.

We have been having a lot of springtime thunderstorms. Three Sundays ago, severe winds blew down trees that pulled down power lines throughout the area. We were without electric power for about 30 hours. Other people were without power for several days. Without electricity we had no lights, no television, only one clock (battery operated), and no computer. The furnace was out and the refrigerator was off. Our electric bill is about $200 per month. The freezers, one in the kitchen and one in the basement, had several hundred dollars worth of frozen food in them. Clearly, we enjoy much more value from electricity than its cost of $200 per month.

My wife and I decided that 1997 was a good time to take our two boys on the vacation of a lifetime. It would not be long before they were too old and involved with their own lives to go on a family vacation, so we decided to go to Hawaii. The roundtrip airfare for the four of us from St. Louis to the Hawaiian island of Kauai was about $3000. That was far less than the cost of travelling any other way. Going by air had far more value to us than the price. The trip would have been impossible by any other means. The cheaper mode of travel was more valuable than a more expensive one.

There were many other people on the same flights with us. Some flew with us from St. Louis to Salt Lake City where they deplaned. Others went on to San Francisco. Another group flew with us from San Francisco to Honolulu. A different group flew with us from Honolulu to the Lihue airport on Kauai. All of those people had their own reasons for traveling. Some were traveling on business and would make a profitable business deal at their destination while others would fail. Some were leaving home; some were returning home. Some were on their first airplane trip and were excited beyond words; others had traveled many times and were bored.

Yet the prices paid for their tickets did not reflect the varied purposes of their travel. Only in exceptional circumstances, for example, a family emergency does the airline care why people are traveling. Their primary concern is filling the plane to cover their costs and make a profit.

These and other considerations that you may think of lead, I believe, to the conclusion that price reflects value only in the sense that we value our time and money and we want value in exchange for them.

What we need to think when the GDP goes up from one year to the next is that we are collectively paying a higher price for what we hope is higher value, though it may not be. I expect that running water and electricity for my family will have the same value next year as it has this year, though we may have to pay more for them.

The proper interpretation of GDP is as Gross Domestic *Price*, insofar as those prices are included in the sum of the selling prices of all goods and services produced in a year. No one can dispute that GDP is calculated by adding the selling prices of all goods and services produced in a year. How something is calculated is the clearest evidence of what it means. We can argue forever about the value of those goods and services, but we cannot argue about the prices for which they sold. Price is usually recorded in sales receipts and income tax returns. There may be some fudging of the books, but by and large sales receipts reflect selling prices.

We begin building the new model for saving time and money by changing the meaning of GDP from Gross Domestic Product to Gross Domestic Price. This single and simple change has profound significance that can improve the practice of economics forever. There are two major implications of the change.

First, as price, GDP becomes what we want to *reduce*, not increase. Given a certain level of product quality, good economics says we should seek ways to reduce price. As a society, then, we should seek ways to reduce the total price we pay each year for goods and services.

Reducing Gross Domestic Price would mean, for example, striving to reduce the number of automobile accidents each year. Fewer accidents would reduce the price those accidents add to GDP. Taking better care of our automobiles so that they can be used for many hundreds of thousands of miles would reduce the price that replacement automobiles add to the Gross Domestic Price. By building our homes and offices to better withstand earthquakes, we could reduce the price that repairing earthquake damage adds to the GDP. By better managing our waterways and our use of land on floodplains, we could reduce the damage caused by flooding. In short, understanding GDP as Gross Domestic Price could start a process of examining every facet of our production and consumption to find ways to improve the quality of goods and services while lowering their prices.

Notice what this change would mean for the environment. By taking better care of what we produce so that it can be used longer, we reduce the need to consume resources to replace it. Our goal of reducing GDP would mean conservation of resources and less production with its attendant pollution. Without trying to put a dollar value on what we waste in trees, minerals, and plant and animal species, we would be changing the direction of economic endeavors to conserve them.

The second implication of understanding GDP as Gross Domestic Price is that we then need a different way of measuring national well being. If we cannot use GDP, what can we use? I have a method that makes good sense to me because I am a sociologist rather than an economist. As such, I know of a measure that is not studied by economists as part of their discipline. That measure is life expectancy.

Chapter 6

Life Expectancy as the Measure of Wealth

Let us reflect a bit on what we want in a measure of national wealth.

First, I think, and I hope you agree, that the measure should reflect real values, that is goods and services that satisfy our material, social, emotional, and intellectual needs and wants. We might each choose different specific items, but they would include in general terms, food, clothing, shelter, safe neighborhoods and friendly neighbors, good schools, competent health care, easy travel and recreation.

These could and probably should be measured in their own terms. For example, if we want to know the wealth of the nation in terms of housing, we count the number of housing units we have and we assess their quality. The Census Bureau does this kind of assessment with the long form of the census and in periodic surveys. If we want to know the food situation, we can measure it in bushels of corn and wheat and heads of chicken, hog, and cattle. This kind of assessment allows us to focus on where specifically we need to make improvements, and it should be a normal and routine planning tool.

Second, I think a desirable characteristic of a measure of national well being is that it should add up to a single summary number. While knowing the state of our housing and our food supply and the number of children enrolled in school can tell us the state of the nation in each particular, it does not produce a single summary benchmark. A good thing about GDP is that it is a single figure. So when the GDP goes up, we can say we did better than last year, or when it goes down, we say the economy is not as healthy as we would like.

Third, I think, a measure of national well being should represent *everyone's* well being insofar as possible. It should avoid the inherent problem of the GDP: failure to reflect the distribution of well being.

The measure that meets these three conditions that I propose replaces GDP to measure the general well being of the nation is *life expectancy*. Life expectancy is a measure developed by demographers and widely used by insurance companies to set life insurance premiums.

Life expectancy is based entirely on death rates for all age groups in a society. If all age groups are doing well, their death rates will be low and life expectancy will be high. If many or all age groups are doing badly, their death rates will be high and life expectancy will be low. Using life expectancy to measure the general condition of a country is like using temperature and blood pressure to measure the general health of the human body. We could measure health by doing many complicated studies of the body with x-rays and blood tests and by surveying people about their diet and life style. However, experience has shown that a person's temperature and blood pressure are good indicators of overall health. These do not preclude other tests, but they often indicate that other tests are not needed.

The same is true of life expectancy. Where it is high, we can safely conclude that people are generally well off. Where it is low, we know there are problems and we should take a closer look at particulars.

Life expectancy is versatile. It can be calculated for any subgroup, as people in the life insurance business can tell you. We can determine life expectancy for males and females, for people in any age group, for people of any ethnic category, and for people in any geographic area of the country.

The new model, one that will achieve the most wealth for the least work, will focus on life expectancy as the measure of well

34

being and Gross Domestic Product as the measure of price. The news that we would then want to hear is, "Life expectancy continues up, while Gross Domestic Price continues down!"

Chapter 7

Wealth for Everyone Through Cooperation

Like good architects, we need to build on a good foundation. The foundation I build on consists of two principles: 1) wealth for everyone, and 2) through cooperation.

First, I hope that we agree on the goal of wealth in the true sense of the word, i.e., being healthy, happy, and wise. When we talk about wealth, it's not gold or silver that we mean. Wealth is food, clothing, shelter, medical care, education, travel, free time, and fun. It's clean air and water. It's freedom from fear, freedom from want, freedom from worry about our own or other people's security. I could elaborate, but you get the general idea.

The second principle of the new model is that we achieve wealth through cooperation. No one can produce wealth alone. We need each other to be healthy, wealthy, and wise. Alone no one could produce even a tiny fraction of all the things we need to be healthy. There is not a person alive who can raise more than a fraction of the variety of vegetables, cereals, proteins, and beverages that make eating healthy and pleasant.

We need many different kinds of farmers, the specialists in food production, to produce that variety. And farmers need seed and fertilizer suppliers, tractor and equipment makers, road, truck, railroad and warehouse builders, package manufacturers, and grocers to distribute the food. Again, I could elaborate, but I think you get the general idea. To put the second principle another way: cooperation produces wealth. Only by working together can we produce the many goods and services we need to be healthy, wealthy, and wise.

A corollary to the second principle is: the larger the scale of cooperation, the greater the wealth produced. Two people can produce more than one; three people can produce more than two; four people can produce more than three. Add any order of magnitude and the principle remains the same. Two hundred people can produce more than one hundred. Three hundred people can produce more than two hundred, and so forth.

The employed labor force of the United States today is 135 million people. It includes tens of thousands of different kinds of specialists. The Republicans and the Democrats can say what they will about why the country is prosperous. I think you would agree with me that the United States is prosperous because of the productive work done by the 135 million people in the paid labor force, plus many people who are not paid at all, such as housewives and schoolchildren.

This is not to say that everyone collecting a paycheck is doing productive work. On the contrary, a basic reason that so many of us are working harder than ever before is that it has become socially necessary to work harder while producing less in order to stay employed. J.W. Smith supports this idea with many examples in his book, *The World's Wasted Wealth 2* (1994).

A few years ago, I overheard a skilled craftsman tell his buddies in a bar that he had not done a good day's work in ten years. No doubt he exaggerated, but most of us could probably identify days when we killed time on the job. Why? We all know the answer. We do not want to reduce our paycheck.

One summer when I was working my way through college, I was employed by a road construction company. About ten of us were assigned to clean concrete off metal rails used in building roads. The work was necessary. We used metal brushes to remove the old concrete, and then each rail was dipped in oil to keep it from rusting and to help minimize the amount of concrete that adhered to the form the next time it was used.

I quickly got the message from my co-workers that we were not to work efficiently. In fact, it was quite the opposite. We were to make a lot of work noise and when the boss came by we were to give him a good show of diligent effort, but the most important goal was to clean as few rails as possible. Why? The answer was simple. We expected that several of us, if not all of us, would be laid off as soon as we were done.

The boss noticed that we were not making much progress so he decided to bring in some new technology, electric grinders. The grinders had round wire brushes that rotated at high speed, a thousand times faster than we could scrape with our handheld wire brushes. Lo and behold, after we began using the electric grinders we cleaned no more rails than we had before. That's right. We accomplished no more work than we had before. When the boss was in the office, out of sight but within earshot, we ran the grinders to make more work noise but without touching them to the rails.

It was fun, at least for a while, playing our little game of "fool the boss," but it made the day terribly boring. Before long, the boss realized what was up and he laid off half the group anyway.

We must cooperate to produce wealth, and we must find a way for the people who do the work to reap the benefit of their own efficiency. Today they often do not. Who among us can go to their boss and say, "Today I want to finish all my work by noon, and then take the rest of the day off? Okay? Of course, I want my full day's pay." What do you think would happen if people could go home as soon as they finished their necessary work?

I think that many people would finish by noon all the work that currently takes all day and then take the rest of the day off!

All it would take is a guarantee that they would still earn a full day's pay. This is an example of what I mean by going beyond repairing to remodeling. People would still have to work for a living, but they could be efficient to a much larger degree than today. The trick is figuring out how to do it, how to empower people to do necessary work better and sooner without any loss of pay. When we figure this one out, we will see our work time dramatically reduced.

To recapitulate, the two principles on which I base the new model are: 1) we all want to be wealthy, and 2) we must cooperate to do it. A design defect in our present system is that we cannot be efficient without fear of losing our jobs. We need to find a way to increase our efficiency without reducing our pay. We want increased efficiency to mean increased pay. In the next three chapters we examine the rules that make cooperation succeed: 1) Communicate, 2) Specialize, and 3) Reciprocate.

Chapter 8

The First Rule of Cooperation: Communicate

To cooperate, people must communicate. We must speak to one another and agree to do our part of what must be done. To reach that agreement, we must have a way to share the necessary information. Our most familiar way to communicate is through language.

Spoken Language

To cooperate, we must speak the same language. The evidence is clear for nations. Where most people speak the same language, the nation is wealthy. Where many languages are spoken, the nation is poor. The average life expectancy is 68 years in nations where more than 90 percent of the people speak the same language. The average life expectancy is 51 years in nations where dozens of different languages are spoken.

Writing

Speaking the same language is not enough. Spoken messages do not travel far before they are distorted and misunderstood. A message repeated from person to person will not get very far along a line of communication before it no longer conveys the same meaning. Cooperation cannot work if people receive distorted or conflicting messages. For cooperation to work, the same message must reach all the people who need it to get the job done well.

Consequently, humans invented writing to increase the reliability of messages and the distance that messages could be successfully relayed. The evolution of writing was one of the great revolutions of progress in human history. Our lives would be primitive without writing.

For most of human life on earth, there was no writing. People communicated by gestures and voice sounds, i.e., short distance media. You must see a gesture to receive a message from it. You must hear a sound to receive a message from it.

Writing increased the distance a message could be sent and, therefore, increased the scale of cooperation. Language with gestures and sounds conveys information accurately only short person-to-person distances.

$$A ---> B ---> C$$

A written message conveys information accurately over a longer person-to-person distance.

$$A ---> B ---> C ---> D ---> E$$

The other night my family and a few friends were vacationing in Kansas City. My wife and I were visiting a friend's house when we received a call on our cell phone that the kids wanted food from McDonald's. The kids were in the hotel room with their friends with their own cell phone. We found a McDonald's and called them for their order. Our son Brian, on the cell phone in the hotel room, had his friends tell him what they wanted. He relayed the orders to my wife on her cell phone, and she relayed the orders to me, and I relayed them through the order microphone to a person inside McDonald's. You can imagine the process and the confusion. After several chains of orders, my wife asked me what my theory of communication would say about what we were doing. I thought for a moment and told her, "It would say what we are trying to do is impossible."

Our first clue that something might be wrong was that the bill was less than we expected. When we got back to the hotel room, we found that we were missing several items. What would have worked better? As you can imagine, we would have been more likely to get every order right by getting each person to write down his or her order and delivering those written notes to the cook at McDonald's. It's a mundane example, but it illustrates how writing can improve cooperation.

Numbers

Numbers are a specialized form of writing. Numbers can communicate messages longer distances than other words because the logic of numbers is simpler. For example, the numbers that mark the location of the pages of this book are simple to follow compared to the complexity of the ideas contained in the words on each page. It is much easier for someone to understand what "page 15" means than to understand any sentence on page 15. In many cases, the message that numbers convey is simply a location, and all one needs to know is the sequence of digits 0, 1, 2, 3, 4, 5, 6, 7, 8, 9. There are more complex uses of numbers, but the simple uses pervade modern life and facilitate large-scale cooperation.

I am sure that you can think of many ways we use numbers to communicate what persons must do to cooperate. Meetings are scheduled with calendars and clocks. The locations of meetings are identified by street, building, floor, and room numbers. Directions to places use numbers for highway routes and miles. Numbers describe the dimensions of things in length, width, and height. Weight, volume, temperature, and strength are designated by numbers. Nutrition labels on food containers use numbers. These and other uses of numbers attest to their universal value in helping people to communicate what they need to know to cooperate.

Money

The key to achieving the most wealth for the least work is understanding money as a medium of communication. Though not normally thought of in this way, money is indeed a medium of communication. Whether it takes the form of coin, paper cash, checks, or electronic transfers by computer, money is denominated in numbers and identified with the author's name and address, whether the author is a government, a corporation, or a person.

When a person hands another person money, they are saying something essential if goods or services are to change hands. People do not ordinarily give up the goods they produce for nothing. Appeals to their humanity only work occasionally. For people to take money as quickly and easily as they do for the groceries, houses, cars, clothing, and thousands of other things that they make, money must talk in a very special way. It must have a message that everyone understands and accepts.

People's understanding of the money message is now in a primitive state. You can check that for yourself by asking anyone to tell you what the money message is. Ask them, "What do you think money says when money talks?"

Let me explain what money does not say. It does not say what you want. For example, when you go into a shoe store, pick the pair you want, and hand the clerk cash, you are not telling the clerk that you want that pair of shoes. He or she knows that you want that pair of shoes because you selected them off the shelf and brought them to the sales counter. Had you presented the money without the shoes, the clerk would have no idea what you wanted.

Furthermore, if the money told the clerk that you wanted the shoes, that would not be a reason for the clerk to give them to you. Clerks don't give customers items because they want them. If that were so, we could simply ask for what we want.

The clerk gives you the shoes in exchange for the money because the clerk knows that he can use that money to get what he wants from other people. That is, money conveys a message to people who are not there. It also gets the message from people who are not there. The first person not there is the person who gave you the money; that person is giving the

44

money message to the person from whom you are buying the shoes. The clerk will pass the money to a fourth person, who is also not there. Just like a written note, money is passing a message from person to person to person to person.

Money's job is to communicate long distance among strangers. Money is a certificate, a printed note with official signs and signatures on it. When person A gives money to person B, person A is sending a certified message to person C saying that person B deserves what B is buying.

Here is how it works. Person A gets the shoes.

A <--shoes-- B

B has given up shoes and has received nothing back. B wants bread, but A is an auto-mechanic, not a baker, so A gives B money certificates instead of bread.

A ----$----> B

B now presents the money certificates to C.

B ----$----> C

C "reads" the money certificates and gives B bread.

B < --bread-- C

Now C has the certificates to pass on to person D for flour to make more bread.

C ----$----> D

D reads the money as certifying that C has done something; D does not need to know what it was to understand that C has the right to the flour.

C <---flour--- D

Now D has the money certificates to pass on to E and on the money goes.

The essential role of money is to pass a certified message among strangers who are absent for part of a transaction. Person A gave the money to B for C who wasn't present for the A—B exchange. Person C used the money to communicate with D, who wasn't present for the B—C exchange. Money certifies that the bearer, stranger though he or she might be, has done something to deserve payment. The real payment is not the money; it is the shoes, the bread, and the flour.

With millions of people cooperating in a complex division of labor, everyone cannot meet together in the same place at the same time. So we use money to span space and time. The person who got the shoes cannot go with the clerk to the bakery to attest that the clerk deserves the bread. So he or she sends the money instead. The money says: "This money certifies that the bearer, or the bearer's benefactor, has performed work equivalent to the amount on this money." As it circulates, money certifies who has earned the right to be paid with goods and services.

The money message, like any other message, may not be true. I included in the message the phrase "or the bearer's benefactor" to cover cases where someone has money that was given to them as a gift. In such cases, the bearer did not earn the right to be paid but obtained the money honestly. In other cases the bearer could be lying. For example, someone who stole the money would be lying.

We have some safeguards against theft. For example, we use complex designs to make counterfeiting difficult. When people pay by personal check we ask for identification like a driver's license. But thefts occur, and thieves who use the money lie in the process, and they cannot be detected because the essence of money is to communicate among strangers.

The graph below summarizes the relationships of spoken language, writing, numbers, and money to the scale of cooperation (specifically, information chain length). Spoken language carries messages accurately short distances. Putting messages into writing increases the distance that they can be conveyed and, therefore, facilitates expansion of the scale of cooperation. Putting messages into numbers increases the distance still more. Putting messages into money carries the message, though ambiguously, the longest distance.

Money authorized by a national government carries messages throughout the nation. Checks authorized by a bank or corporation travel throughout the network of people who recognize and trust that bank or corporation. Personal checks travel between strangers when such things as a driver's license or credit card certify the identity of the author. Money circulates around and around through many hands, never stopping except when it becomes worn and torn. Then the bills are replaced with new ones that continue money's job of long distance communication.

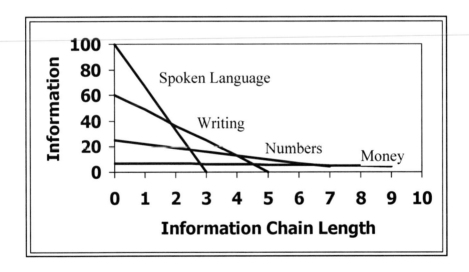

People can lie with money as they can with any message. Lying with money is not limited to thieves. With the money we use today, everyone lies to some degree because the numbers on money are undefined. We cannot tell the truth because we do not know to what "dollar" refers. That is the cause of most money mischief. Because the denominator "dollar" is undefined, people deceive and are deceived about how much they pay and are paid for goods and services. To save money and ourselves from money mischief, we must define its denominator with the same clarity as we define units of length, volume, and weight.

Chapter 9

The Second Rule of Cooperation: Specialize

The power of cooperation increases dramatically with specialization. Specialization allows people to become experts. Experts can do work more effectively and efficiently than non-experts. Each of us could not live well alone because we could not become an expert at much of anything. Together each of us can do his or her special part, which adds up collectively to a cornucopia of expertise.

However, specialization makes communication across specialties difficult. Specialists in the same occupation communicate in a distinct language. Physicians and auto-mechanics speak very different specialized languages. In order for cooperation to include many different kinds of specialists, there must be a language common to all. Specialization also makes it difficult to know when an exchange is reciprocal: What is a fair exchange of apples and oranges? Money can solve these problems.

Money is a language that all specialists speak. In the words of Marshall McLuhan:

> Like words and language, money is a storehouse of communally achieved work, skill, and experience...Even today money is a language for translating the work of the farmer into the work of the barber, doctor, engineer, or plumber. As a vast social metaphor, bridge, or translator, money—like writing—speeds up exchange and tightens the bonds of interdependence in any community. It gives great spatial extension and control to political organization, just as writing does, or the calendar. It is action at a distance,

> both in space and in time. In a highly
> literate…society, 'Time is money,' and money is
> the store of other people's time and effort
> (McLuhan, *Understanding Media: Extensions of
> Man,* 1964:136).

Not only does money talk, it is multilingual. Corporations may have thousands of employees doing hundreds of different kinds of jobs. No one on earth could manage such corporations without money. Money presents, in a simple form, the significant facts on which management can make important decisions. In its early years, General Motors learned the hard way the importance of money as a management tool when it was on the verge of bankruptcy.

The managers of General Motors thought that their job was to oversee the development of automobiles. Because it was an automobile company, it seemed logical for its leaders to be automobile experts. They were wrong. Their first job was to control the budget. In his autobiography, longtime GM executive Alfred Sloan explains:

> Financial method is so refined today that it may
> seem routine; yet this method—the financial
> model, as some call it—by organizing and
> presenting the significant facts about what is going
> on in and around a business, is one of the chief
> bases for strategic business decisions. At all
> times, and particularly in times of crisis, or of
> contraction or expansion from whatever cause, it is
> of the essence in the running of a business (Sloan,
> *My Years With General Motors,* 1963:118).

Given its central importance, imagine the mischief money causes for corporate managers while its unit remains ambiguous. Just as a jet aircraft would behave erratically if its instruments were defective, so business decisions today sometimes have perverse results because their most important decision-making instrument, money, is defective.

Specialization also makes it difficult to define equivalence between things. How can apples be exchanged with oranges? How can the work of a store clerk be compared to that of a truck driver? Money's job of long distance communication requires that its denominator refer to a quality that all specialties share in common. Money's denominator must be a *common* denominator, something shared by shoes, bread, flour, and every other good or service exchanged for money. Without a common denominator, the third rule of cooperation, reciprocate, cannot be honored.

Chapter 10

The Third Rule of Cooperation: Reciprocate

To reciprocate means to exchange equivalent for equivalent. A reciprocal exchange is a fair exchange. Reciprocity is so important to enduring social relationships that it should be regarded as a natural social law. A non-reciprocal relationship is one where one person gives more than they receive. While such imbalance can occur on occasion, any one of us would probably not want to remain in a relationship where we always gave more than we received.

Reciprocity is essential not only in human relationships but elsewhere as well. Walking requires the reciprocal action of each of our legs. Should one leg be longer than the other, we would limp, which makes walking difficult and inefficient. A wonderful example of reciprocity is the wheel. Each segment of a wheel, in turn, carries the weight of the vehicle.

The smoothness and efficiency of the ride depends on the equality of the spokes. One spoke longer than the other would cause a bump and loss of energy as well as unnecessary wear and tear on the wheel supports and cargo.

As with wheels, societies work better when work and wealth are shared equally. Countries where incomes are distributed more equally are wealthier than countries where incomes are distributed more unequally. For example, in Brazil, where the top 20 percent of households receives two thirds of the income, life expectancy is 63. On the other hand, in Norway where the top 20 percent of households receive one third of the income, life expectancy is 75.

The link between income equality and national wealth makes sense in terms of both supply and demand. Consider supply. Greater income equality indicates fuller employment. The scale of cooperation is large; specialization is highly developed; work is effective and efficient. Therefore, there is a large supply of quality goods and services.

On the demand side, greater income equality means more households have the money to buy what they need, what economists call "effective demand." Although a millionaire has a lot of money, he or she has needs and wants not much different from any other human being: good food, nice clothing, and a comfortable home. The millionaire's money does not represent effective demand because the millionaire can eat only about as much food and wear only about as much clothing as any other person.

Distribute a million dollars to a thousand households as $1,000 in additional income and you increase effective demand by the entire million dollars. Many families could find unmet needs to fill with $1,000.

When we find income distributed almost equally in a country, we are probably looking at a country with a good supply of quality commodities that people can afford to buy. When we find income distributed unequally, we are probably looking at a country with a small supply of luxury items that only a few households can afford to buy.

As money passes from hand to hand in long distance lines of communication, its job is to keep exchanges reciprocal. Each person should receive an equivalent of what they give up. The equivalence should pass accurately from person A to person B to person C to person D. The distance money must carry its message of reciprocity is very long. To say that money circulates is to signify how far the money message travels.

Today, because the money denominator is undefined, reciprocity is achieved mostly by accident, but achieving it should be no more difficult than having everyone use the same length for a yard or meter, no matter how often a note expressed in yards or meters changes hands. To improve money reciprocity, we must define the money unit with the same clarity and exactness that we define the yard and the meter.

The kind of money we use today makes reciprocity difficult to achieve because the money denominator is undefined. To what unit of measure does "dollar" refer? A central role of government is to set standards for all weights and measures, including a standard for the money unit. The U.S. Congress has failed to set a standard for "dollar."

Economists are not bothered by this failure because they believe that such a standard cannot be found. Because they think it is impossible, they let the invisible hand of the market determine the value of money. We all know the results: mostly inflation, sometimes deflation, always haggling over wages, salaries, and raises. We would not tolerate letting the market determine our measures of length, volume, and weight, and we should not tolerate it with that most important measure of all, money.

The other day, as I was pumping gas into my car's tank, I noticed a tag on one of the other pumps. It stated that that pump was not accurate. It specified a date by which the pump needed to be corrected. Today, every dollar in circulation, and every form of money in the world, should carry a similar warning: "This money is not accurate because it has no definite unit of measure." Imagine how quickly people would demand that this defect be corrected!

Chapter 11

The Role of Government: Define the Ruler

"To rule" has two meanings. The one we generally think of is to govern. In this meaning, government rules by making laws that limit our behavior. But rule also means to measure. We rule when we use that stick for measuring that we call a ruler. This is not coincidence. Government rules best (and least) by setting standards of weight and measure. Once these standards are properly defined, people are able to rule themselves.

In the contemporary debate over the role of government, some people argue that government should be all but abolished. They believe that government cannot make good policies and that individuals in their private lives are better able to decide what is best for them. They claim that government merely burdens private citizens with excessive rules and regulations. Other people argue that government is essential and that without it there would be chaos. Understanding the importance of standards helps resolve the debate.

Communication with language, writing, numbers, and money is greatly improved by standardization. Standards ensure that everyone understands words and numbers in the same way. Standards define correct use and meaning. Standards take away the freedom to invent our own language in exchange for the power to communicate accurately and efficiently. Standards make a language a common one.

Printing exemplifies standardization. Each time the letter "a" occurs on this page, it is exactly the same. Printers are not free to make "a" look like anything else. This exactness makes it easy for you and everyone else who knows English to read the words on this page. The meaning of words is also standardized.

Dictionaries report accepted standards of word spellings and meanings.

The essential role of government is to set standards. The United States federal government in Washington, D.C. maintains national standards for length, volume, weight and many scientific units. The Constitution gives Congress the duty to regulate the value of money. The best way to perform that duty would be to set a standard for "dollar." The First Congress defined the dollar in terms of a weight of gold and silver. It was correct in using a thing; it was incorrect in the thing it used.

A standard of measure is always an object. It is a thing, something physical, so that it can be felt, seen, heard, tasted, or smelled. The standard for the British yard is the distance between two gold studs in a bar of platinum kept in London. The standard defines, or makes definite, the magnitude of the unit. The standard leaves no doubt or ambiguity about the unit because people can match their measuring sticks with the standard to ensure accuracy.

When a government properly defines standards, citizens of the country are free to make their own use of them. Defining standards shifts responsibility for ruling from government to private citizens. The debate over the role of government is resolved by identifying which decisions are best made by individuals and which decisions are best made by government.

It is best that government set standards. Once those standards are set, individual people can make their own decisions applying those standards. For this reason we call the stick we use for measuring length a ruler.

When we use a ruler to measure length, the ruler governs length. When buying something that involves length, such as cloth, lumber, or land, one person may judge it to be longer or shorter than another person may. In the absence of a government-defined standard, they could argue over it indefinitely. With a government standard, the dispute is resolved easily and quickly by measuring the length with the ruler. The ruler decides the issue fairly to everyone's satisfaction. Government sets the standard; individuals use it according to their preferences. The government does not tell individuals how much cloth, lumber, or land to buy.

Here we come to the most important idea for achieving the most wealth for the least work. Although the government sets many standards of weight and measure, it does not set a standard for the most important one, namely, a dollar. While the government tells everyone precisely the length of a meter, the volume of a liter, and the weight of a gram, it nowhere defines the value of a dollar. It tells us only that pieces of paper of a certain kind are dollar bills. It is this omission that is at the root of money mischief.

The mischief to which I refer is perhaps most obvious with wages and salaries. Some people are paid a few dollars per hour while others are paid thousands of dollars per hour. In recent years, CEOs of companies have laid off thousands of workers and then given themselves large raises and shares of stock. Steven Forbes, a recent candidate for U.S. President, inherited hundreds of millions of dollar from his father, Malcolm Forbes. These outrageous amounts of money do not seem outrageous because their real meaning is unclear. We know that a million dollars is a lot of money but precisely how much?

Why are some working people required to live on a minimum wage, while some people get millions of dollars for little or no work at all? Some people argue that the reason is value. What the person on minimum wage is doing, we are expected to believe, is less valuable than what the millionaire is doing. This is debatable. What did Steven Forbes do to deserve the hundreds of millions he inherited? Football players would still play if they were paid a fraction of what they are paid. People like football, but it is not necessary to life as are food, water, and shelter. Yet the people who supply food, water, and shelter are often paid minimum wage while athletes are paid millions of dollars for playing a game. It's not fair. That unfairness exists, in my view, because the government has set no standard for the unit of money that we call a dollar.

Bill Gates is one of the richest people in the world. He is said to be worth many billions of dollars. One billion dollars owned by one person is an absurd amount of money, yet it happens because the absurdity of it is not clear. It becomes clear when we express it in real terms, which is what we do with GDP per hour.

Chapter 12

A World Money Standard: An Hour of Work

A proper standard for the money denominator must have the same four features as all standards of weight and measure:

1) It must be an object, an observable physical quantity.

2) It must have the quality for which it is the standard.

3) It must be the same in all places.

4) It must be the same at all times.

The thing that meets these conditions for the money denominator is work time. The central feature of economics to optimize lifetime is using work time to denominate the value of money. We save time and money by marrying them to form *Time Money*.

Intuitively, the marriage makes sense. How many times have you heard people refer to time and money in the same breath? We save time and save money. We spend time and spend money. We invest time and invest money. We seem never to have enough time or enough money. This constant association in our minds of time and money is more than just coincidence. The two belong together.

Time and money organize modern life. Where would we be without clocks and calendars or cash, checks, and credit cards? Notice today how often you use one of these devices to do something. From the time the alarm goes off in the morning to the time we turn off the TV and go to bed at night, we use time and money to make our way through the day. To eat, to work, and to play, we get there and do it on time with money.

The new model for saving time and money defines the money unit with work time. We convert or calibrate each existing money in the world to its equivalent in work time by simple arithmetic.

<u>Gross Domestic Product</u>
Total Hours of Work

We begin with the Gross Domestic Product, the sum of the selling prices of all the goods and services produced in a year. GDP is the total price of goods and services expressed in money.

Money price is not the real price we pay for goods and services. Money price simply *represents* the human price we paid and, therefore, the price we have a right to receive from the persons who want what we produce. Money price is our way of expressing the socially fair price. The fair price is the price that we would have to pay even in a world where money did not exist. Were there no money, the social price would remain. The social price is the price that one person owes another person for something done for his benefit.

Before money was invented, people had to pay a price for goods and services. Goods and services have never been free. Food must be grown; houses must be built; cloth must be woven; and clothing must be sewn. So what is the price that must always and everywhere be paid for goods and services? It is labor. No labor equals no goods.

Some people say that the best things in life are free. That's certainly true of a beautiful sunset or a cool sunlit twilight sky. But very few things are free. Water is rarely free. It must be pumped from wells or rivers, sanitized, and piped to offices and homes. Air is free on a good day, but it must be heated in winter and cooled in summer. As Adam Smith (1723-1790) wrote in his 1776 classic, *The Wealth of Nations*:

> The real price of everything, what everything really costs to the man who wants to acquire it, is the toil and trouble of acquiring it. What everything is really worth to the man who has

acquired it, and who wants to dispose of it or exchange it for something else, is the toil and trouble which it can save to himself, and which it can impose upon other people...Labor was the first price, the original purchase-money that was paid for all things. It was not by gold or by silver, but by labor, that all the wealth of the world was originally purchased (Adam Smith, *The Wealth of Nations*, 1963: 24; Originally published in 1776.).

Labor is the price that we should be representing with money.

A mistake today is equating money price to value rather than to price. Money is not a measure of value; it can only represent price. As I explained earlier, the values of food, clothing, travel, medical care, and education are like beauty; they are in the eyes of the beholder. The value of apples and oranges cannot be compared; only their prices can be compared because both require a common denominator to be produced, namely, labor.

Capitalism confuses price with value. It is used to justify charging more than labor price. The capitalist equation for profit is:

$$Price - Cost = Profit$$

Profit is then the difference between what I paid for something and the money I get when I sell it. What the equation does not show is that my profit is someone else's loss. Understand that cost should include any expenses I incurred, including my own labor. Only after all costs are included can there be profit. If I am charging more than everything I paid, the buyer is paying more than the total cost of the item.

We have sayings that warn buyers that they are likely to suffer a loss. One saying is "buy cheap and sell dear." Another is the Latin, *caveat emptor*, or beware buyer. In truth, cost is nothing more than price by another name. So the equation can also be written:

$$Price - Price = Profit$$

Written this way, there is no justification for profit. So price had to be redefined to mean value. By that definition, sellers and buyers are in competition with each other. Sellers want the highest possible prices while buyers want the lowest possible prices. Neither talks to the other about the fair, socially appropriate price.

In an economics that aims at the most wealth for the least work, the fair price is labor time and profit is time saved. We repay the producer for the work they did to produce an item. We then own the item to use as we want. Profit is the difference between the time we worked to earn the money we used to buy an item and the time we now have to use it. Real profit is free time, the difference between the time that a good or service can be used and the work time required to produce it:

$$Use time - Work time = Free time (real profit).$$

If money represents the price we owe the producer, then the appropriate object-standard for money is the work time price. With it in place, we can realize real profit, increased free time.

All types of work share the common denominator of work time. Everywhere we measure work by observed work time. That is, a person is hired to do a job, and the person who hires them supervises, watches, and observes the work being done. The employer may not watch every minute of work. He or she may choose to look in on the worker from time to time and/or may judge the efficacy of the work by the quality of the final product. If the final product is satisfactory, the employer pays the employee. That act of payment certifies the bearer as being entitled to payment for work done. The employee then takes the money to a third party who accepts the money certificate and gives the bearer the good or service.

Work time has all the qualities needed for a money standard.

1) Work time is observable.

2) It has the quality for which it would serve as standard, the real price for goods and services.

3) An hour of work is an hour in all places.

4) An hour is the same time at all times.

Individuals may vary in how long they take to do the same job. The same job may take different amounts of work depending on tools used or time of day. A person with a bulldozer can move more earth in an hour than a person with a pick and shovel. Restaurant work is most intense at mealtimes. These kinds of variations can be handled. Keep in mind the comparison with the ruler measuring stick. While the length of the ruler remains the same, people can use discretion in deciding how much length of land or cloth to buy or sell.

Consider the bulldozer example. The bulldozer cost labor to produce: the work time to build it, from mining iron ore to bolting it together; the work time to fuel it and maintain it; the work time to deliver it to the site; the work time to train the operator; and the work time to use it. All such costs need to be included in the work time to move the earth. Still we expect that the total cost of having the dirt moved by bulldozer is less than the cost of a man doing it with a pick and shovel. Otherwise, why would we use bulldozers? In short, once the components of the machine and the operator are broken down and factored in, we get the price. The price of the bulldozer and operator is the total price of all its components.

Think about the restaurant example. While it is true that restaurant work is most intense at mealtime, employers employ workers throughout the day at the same wages. So workers work very intensely at mealtime, but during other parts of the day they work at a more leisurely pace. Their pay should reflect the average amount of work done. It is possible to vary the pay by work intensity, but that would add unnecessary bookkeeping. Instead, workers are paid for their effort on the average.

Variations from individual to individual can also be taken into account. New hires can be paid half time during their training period. Exceptionally good workers can be paid time-and-a-half. Work on holidays can be paid double-time. The essential difference between how wages are decided today and how they could be decided to achieve the most wealth for the least work is in the clarity of the money unit.

Today the dollar is undefined and unstable. Negotiating wages, salaries, and raises requires a lot of guess and bluff. No one really knows what he or she is talking about when they talk dollars. With hour money the real meaning of the money is clear: work time measured by the clock and calendar.

Given the theory, how do we establish the value of today's dollars in terms of work time? We take today's Gross Domestic Product and divide it by the total hours of work that produced it. Here is where the simple arithmetic comes in.

The *Statistical Abstract* of *the United States* for 2002 reports the Gross Domestic Product in 2001 as $10.2 trillion produced by 132 million workers working an average of 34.2 hours per week. At that rate over 50 weeks per year, they worked an average of 34.2 times 50 weeks = 1,710 hours. Therefore, the total hours worked was 132 million times 1,710 = 225.7 billion hours.

Therefore, the GDP per hour of work was:

$10,208/ 225.7 = $45.23 per hour of work

GDP expresses the price in money of what was produced. Hours worked expresses the price in labor. Therefore, in 2001 the value of the US dollar in work time was $45.23 per hour.

How much was labor actually paid to produce this GDP? It was paid an average hourly wage of $14.33. Labor produced the GDP at the rate of $45.23 but was paid at the rate of $14.33, 32 percent of what labor produced. Where did the other 68 percent go? In various ways, it went to people who did no actual work to produce the GDP. It went to corporations through the mechanism of depreciation allowances, to landlords in the form of rents, to owners of stock as dividends, and to owners of money in the form of interest. One can argue about whether or not these owners should receive a share of the product and what that share might be. The problem is that the share, as far as I know, is never defined. Does labor know that its share has declined? Does capital know that its share has increased? Has either party discussed what would be a fair share?

The share that goes to labor has declined steadily since 1960. In 1960, labor received an average wage per hour of $2.09 on a GDP per hour of $4.04, a 52 percent share. From 1960 to 2001 the average hourly wage rose from $2.09 to $14.33, an apparent gain for workers, but their share of the product dropped from 52 percent to 32 percent. What allowed this drop to occur? The ambiguity of the dollar!

Put another way, GDP is the pie. If the wage rate had been defined in relation to the size of the pie, people producing the pie would probably have insisted on a fair share. Whatever share fair might be, a declining share would not have been tolerated. But annual raises created the impression that labor's share was growing. Such is the mischief of an undefined money unit.

Besides fairness, there is also the issue of the functioning of the economy. When the income of a large segment of the population falls from a 52 percent share to a 32 percent share, effective demand declines. Money paid in wages becomes money in the hands of consumers. The decline in GDP share to workers meant a decline in consumer purchasing power. Two malfunctions then occur: 1) More goods and services remain unsold, and 2) Buyers must borrow to buy so that consumer debt increases. Like a car running out of gas, the economy sputters and gasps.

Increased consumer debt is especially troublesome because debt carries the burden of compound interest. The decline in purchasing power with this systematic drop in GDP share means less money to pay consumer debt. Interest on that debt compounds and solvency plummets. We tend to focus on the explosion in federal debt, but the problem exists throughout the economy. Explosions in debt have occurred for farmers, state and local governments, and corporations as well as for households and the federal government. Keeping wages in line with the GDP per hour would at least increase the purchasing power of households. The problem of exploding debt requires a different approach, which we will take up in a later chapter.

Defining the value of money as GDP per hour is the first step toward true Hour Money. Ultimately, the numbers printed on money would represent work time. Such a money form is already in use. Edgar Cahn and Jonathan Rowe (1992) describe the use of Time Dollars by senior citizens to increase their purchasing power, personal security, and community renewal. People in Ithaca, New York have the most advanced form of time money. They denominate their money in hours that they call Ithaca Hours.

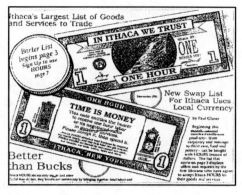

They have hours, half hours, quarter hours, and one-eighth hours. When someone does work for someone else they are paid Ithaca Hours about equal to the length of time they work. I say "about equal" because the people completing the transaction decide exactly how much is paid for a certain amount of work.

Because Ithaca is in the United States and the US currency is denominated in dollars, the people governing the issue of Ithaca Hours had to define an exchange rate for Ithaca Hours relative to US dollars. They decided that $10 dollars per Ithaca Hour was reasonable. Now people buy and sell with combinations of dollars and Hours. You can find Ithaca Hours on the Internet by typing in "ithacahours" as a search word.

The limitation of Ithaca Hours is that they are acceptable only within the Ithaca Hour network. For people to buy beyond that network, they need dollars, and hence, the need for an exchange rate. That raises the general matter of exchange rates. How would using GDP per hour to define the US dollar affect its value relative to other national currencies?

Exchange rates are needed when buying and selling goods across national boundaries. For example, people in Canada buy US goods with Canadian dollars in Canada. The merchants who sell those goods in Canada must then take the Canadian dollars they receive from sales to a bank where they exchange them for US dollars. Then they use the US dollars to buy more goods from US suppliers for sale in Canada. The Canadian dollar exchange rate varies. This fluctuation occurs because neither the Canadian dollar nor the US dollar is defined. No one knows what either one is worth. This uncertainty causes the value of both currencies to rise and fall. One day the news from Canada is bad; for example, the French in Quebec want to secede and form their own country so the value of the Canadian dollar falls. The day after the vote on secession, the value of the Canadian dollar rises again.

Did the vote alter the length of the Canadian meter relative to the US meter? Not at all. Why not? They are both defined in terms of a fixed, standard physical length.

For the same reason, if Canadian money had been denominated in Hours and US money had been denominated in Hours, the election would have had no effect on the exchange rate between Canadian Hours and US Hours. The election had nothing to do with the length of the clock hour. Indeed, whatever the outcome of the election, the Hour would be unchanged. If Quebec had become a separate country, it could have issued its money denominated in Hours and it could have exchanged Quebec Hours for Canadian Hours and US Hours at a precise Hour-for-Hour rate.

Today, no national currency in the world is denominated in hours. Instead, we have a Babel of money units as varied as languages. The result is similar to having people of a country speaking dozens of distinct languages, namely, less wealth and more work. Cooperation can extend only as far as people can understand one another. Beyond that range, cooperation falters in misunderstanding.

Gross Domestic Product per hour provides a way to end the mess with exchange rates in a language that everyone understands, work time. The simple division of GDP by hours worked can be done for every country in the world. The result would be clear, fair, and stable exchange rates for money. Each country would exchange their money for any other country's money at the rate of one hour for one hour.

Today exchange rates are far from simple. Instead, rich countries buy the money, and therefore the goods, of poor countries for pennies on the dollar. Poor countries, on the other hand, cannot afford to buy from rich countries. Instead, they work for pennies per hour. Not only is this unfair, it also causes employers to move their plants from high wage countries to low wage countries.

Again we have malfunction but on a global level. Rich countries have rising unemployment because of below cost imports, while poor countries have rising employment for poverty wages. Working harder does not work in either situation. Workers in rich countries cannot arrest the flight of jobs because they cannot accept poverty wages. Workers in poor countries cannot buy a higher standard of living because they are hostage to unfair currency exchange rates.

By adopting GDP per hour as the exchange rate standard, job flight would stop. Immediately, reality could operate as it should. In many cases, perhaps most, it is cheaper to produce goods locally rather than to transport goods thousands of miles. The labor time to produce shoes in the U.S. is probably about the same as the labor time to produce shoes in China. With wages worldwide equalized to an hour of money for an hour of work, it would make sense to produce and sell shoes locally instead of adding the cost of transoceanic transportation.

The effect on the world economy would be similar to the effect of equalizing blood flow in a human body. Today the world economy is hemorrhaging; some parts are awash in more goods than they can use while others are drained of essential food and materials. Stop the hemorrhaging and the world can become healthy.

Although no nation today denominates its money in hours, work time underlies more than 85 percent of the exchange rate of national monies. The hour is working invisibly to make exchange rates fairer than they would be otherwise.

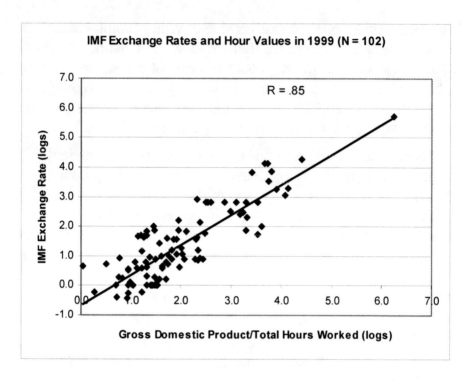

You can see on the graph how closely countries aligned with exchange rates equivalent to equal work time in 1999. Experts in the field have not recognized this relationship, as far as I know. It suggests that work time is the center of gravity of exchange rates. The same strong relationship between actual currency exchange rates and those that would exist if currencies were calibrated to equal amounts of work time has existed for as long as the International Monetary Fund has published exchanged rates. Whatever might be the theory, the reality is that work time has exerted its influence powerfully and persistently.

Chapter 13

GDP per Hour as a Wage Standard

Is it fair to pay people an hour of money for an hour of work? Is a fair wage a day's pay for a day's work? Should people be paid by the hour, by the day, by the week, and by the year? The question is almost humorous. Are not people already paid by the hour, day, week, and year? Why? It is a practical and moral way to pay them.

Paying people on a regular basis according to the passage of time on a clock and a calendar is practical. Doing so means that everyone knows when to pay and when to be paid. It makes pay predictable. People can plan their lives accordingly. Most expenditures are periodic. Rent or mortgage payments come due monthly, as do utility and credit card bills. Knowing when they will be paid means that people know when to buy groceries and how much to buy. Paying people on time makes life manageable. What makes life manageable is practical, and it makes moral sense to treat people that way.

Imagine the opposite. Would it be fair if employers never paid their employees on a regular schedule? Would it be fair if landlords could demand rent payments at any time? Would it be fair if banks could demand mortgage payments at any time? Not at all. We would think of them as capricious if not malicious.

The big question is: Is it fair to pay every kind of job by the same standard, an hour of money for an hour of work. What about the job that requires expensive training? What about the job that involves high risk? What about the job that requires initiative or creativity? What about the person who works diligently the entire time compared to the person who does little or nothing until prodded? What about the person of rare talent? Should these and other relevant variations be ignored?

Let's go back to the example of measuring length with a ruler. Because the foot is always the same, must all clothes come in lengths of exactly one foot, no shorter and no longer? Must all lumber be the same length? Must all land be the same size? Clearly not. While the standard must remain the same, its application can vary with circumstances. Clothing for a child is smaller than clothing for an adult. Lumber used for the walls of a building are shorter than lumber used for roof rafters. Land area for a shopping mall is larger than land area for a house.

Similarly, the pay for work can vary with things such as training, risk, diligence, talent, and initiative. If a person is twice as productive as someone else in the same period of time, that person should be paid twice as much. If a person paid to go to school to develop the skills for doing a job, that cost should be included in the pay. If equipment had to be bought, if the job is high risk, these elements should also be included in determining the pay rate.

Money denominated in hours should be used as other units of weight and measure are used. The government defines the standard; people apply the standard according to their knowledge of the situation. This may seem like the way things are done now, but it is not.

The crucial difference is that today wage and salary negotiations go on with no standard unit. People throw dollar numbers around that are ridiculous when converted to hours. A movie actress was recently paid 12 million dollars for her part in a movie. Let's be generous and say that she worked 12 hours a day, 6 days a week, for 26 weeks to make the movie. That would come to 12 x 6 x 26 = 1872 hours. Let's round it up to 2,000 hours in case we forgot some time. Her pay then was $12,000,000/2,000 = $6,000 per hour. Denominated in dollars, this will seem to some readers as a lot of money and to other readers as not that much money, especially if they saw the movie and thought that she was really good.

Let's now convert her pay to hours. At the 2001 GDP per hour rate of $45.23, how many hours are represented by $12 million? $12,000,000/$45.23 = 265,310 hours. At the full-time rate of 40 hours per week for 50 weeks, or 2,000 hours, that pay for a movie was 133 years. No matter how good she was, does 133 years of pay for making a movie now seem reasonable? Notice that the calculation was done using $45.23 per hour. The average hourly wage paid other workers was only $14.33. At that rate $12 million equals 837,404 hours, or 419 years.

What about the pay for nurses, police, fire fighters, schoolteachers, and school bus drivers? Is it fair that one movie actress should receive centuries of pay while other jobs that save lives every day are paid much less than $30 per hour?

I don't mean to pick on an actress. Consider the football quarterback who will be paid $42 million over 7 years. At $45.23 per hour, that amounts to 464 years of income at $90,460 per year.

With GDP per hour as a wage standard, exceptional people, whether actresses or football players, could be paid exceptional salaries, but they would be more reasonable than at present. Pay them double or triple what a fire fighter or nurse makes, but not hundreds of times more. Everyone would be better off.

No one needs millions of dollars to be wealthy, healthy, and wise. The opposite probably happens. And consider the political implications of having millionaires and billionaires. Money is power. Democracy cannot exist where some people have millions and others have no discretionary income. Political democracy can survive only on a foundation of economic democracy. GDP per hour as a wage standard is the economic equivalent of the political standard, One Person, One Vote.

Chapter 14

GDP per Hour as a Price Standard

GDP is obtained by summing the selling prices of all goods and services produced in a year. It expresses the total price of goods and services produced in a year. It represents what we collectively pay to produce goods and services. GDP per hour is the price we pay per hour. To use GDP per hour as a price standard is to apply the price at each point of sale.

For example, if something required one hour to produce, counting everything that went into the process of production including raw material, equipment, and labor, then its price equals GDP per hour. With GDP per hour at $45.23, its selling price should be $45.23. If it required 4 hours to produce, its selling price should be $180.92.

Economists interpret GDP as the total value of goods and services. This is another way that mischief enters the money picture. If price represents value, then it is appropriate to charge more for things that people value more and less for things they value less. An example is medical care. Anyone with a life threatening condition values medical care to the ultimate degree. Therefore, according to the price = value interpretation, they can expect to pay a very high price for that care. Anyone who has had medical care lately knows that it has become hugely expensive.

The same has happened in elder care facilities. The savings of a lifetime can be consumed in a few years paying for room and board. Heart bypass surgery costs hundreds of thousands of dollars. If you have a toothache you could pay anywhere from $50 to $500. Why? We are held hostage by our needs.

Value governs the price of homes. People need shelter; therefore, housing prices have gone up for generations. The house I live in was built in 1910. The person who had it built lived here until he died in 1945. At that time it was valued at $2,000. The person I bought it from paid $10,000 for it in 1965. I bought it in 1968 for $17,500. The houses in my neighborhood in 2003 are selling for more than $100,000. I could get at least that much for this house.

If I were talking to a prospective buyer, I would probably not tell him or her anything about the history of the price of this house. Instead, I would emphasize that I built three rooms upstairs in what had been the attic. I would let them appreciate the 9 and 1/2 foot ceilings on the first floor and the lovely park and lake directly across the street. I would point out that the elementary school is just two blocks away. Notice that everything I would mention pertains to value, not to price. In this behavior I think I would be typical of other house sellers. But I would be cheating the prospective buyer because I would be saying nothing about the price I paid, only the price I want them to pay. That would be wrong.

Look how I would be unfair. For one thing, I would not be factoring into price the 35 years that I have lived in this house. I would not be factoring in that the house is now 93 years old. This house should be cheaper today than it was the day it was finished.

I live in the Midwest where housing is cheaper than on the East or West Coast. In Southern California, a couple bought a 1400 square foot house in San Diego County in 1978 for $45,000. One of their children bought a similar house in the same city in 2000 for $199,000. They are all track houses built in the early 1970s!

All houses should be less expensive as they get older. The opposite happens because the way houses are priced today, we must cheat each other in order to reduce the amount that we are cheated when we buy the next house we live in. To defend ourselves, we pass aging houses and huge mortgages on to each other. The profits exist only on paper. The reality is an overpriced and deteriorating housing stock with families overworking to pay excessive mortgages. Setting prices at work time would enable housing prices to decrease as houses age.

As a house ages, the work that produced it must be re-produced to repair wear and tear. The home resident uses up that work time and so should accept a lower price than they paid—if they failed to maintain the house—or the same price they paid if they maintained it. Of course, if they added improvements to the house, it would be fair to repay them for the improvements depreciated for the time they used the improvements.

If housing prices remained stable or declined, it would give buyers a lot of money to maintain a newly acquired house. Our housing stock would get older but would remain in good repair as mortgage debt declined. We can live with that scenario; the one we use now is killing us.

Chapter 15
The Annual Review

At the same time each year, the government could review the Gross Domestic Price/Total Hours Worked relationship. They could then announce the new GDP per hour standard. Suppose this had been public policy for the past 13 years.

In 1990 the GDP per hour was $27.27. Therefore, for 1991 the federal government would have announced $27.27 per hour as the National Wage and Price Standard. Everyone could then have negotiated their wages and salaries and the prices they paid for goods and services in terms of that rate. Some could have negotiated a higher rate while others could have accepted a lesser rate based on whatever factors they brought to the negotiation.

Then, in 1991 when new data became available, the government would have conducted its annual review. Then GDP per hour would have increased to $28.56, which could have been announced as the new National Wage and Price Standard. This would have meant that workers could expect an average raise of $1.29 per hour. Some might receive a larger raise and some might receive a smaller raise, depending on work quality and negotiations with their employers, but all of us would have talked the same language—the language of hour money.

Each year the federal government would have conducted its annual review. In 1992, the National Wage and Price Standard would have been $29.76; in 1993, it would have been $30.82; in 1994, it would have been $31.56.

As wages were adjusted in line with changes in GDP per hour, prices would also be adjusted. Average price per hour would have risen in five years from $27.27 per hour of production time to $31.56, a rise of $4.56 per hour.

What in fact happened from 1991 to 1994? The average wage went up from $10.01 to $11.13, a raise of $1.12 per hour over five years. Labor worked for only a third of what labor produced and gained only a quarter of the rise in prices. In this way labor's share of production since 1950 has dropped from 50 percent to 30 percent with no end in sight.

We are accustomed to prices always moving upward. This is the reverse of what we should expect. The normal direction for prices should be down. There are two main and simple reasons for this. First, development costs for new products are high. As sales increase and production volume increases, price per unit comes down. Second, once something is produced, it is cheaper to maintain it than to reproduce it.

I bought my first computer in 1982. It was an Apple II+. It had 48,000 bytes of random access memory (RAM) and an external disk drive that ran 5 1/4 inch floppy disks each with about 330,000 bytes of storage space, and it was attached to an Epson dot-matrix printer. The keyboard had no movement keys. When I hit the escape key twice, the keys I, J, K, and M became movement keys for small movements, and the keys E, S, D, and X became movement keys for larger movements. It had no mouse, and the monitor was monochrome. The system cost me $3,100.

The computer I have now has 256 million bytes of RAM, an 80 billion byte hard drive, a DVD/CD writer and reader with upwards of 650 million bytes of storage, a 3.5 inch floppy drive with disks that have 1.4 million bytes of storage space, separate movement keys, and 12 function keys. I am connected to the Internet by cable; my monitor is a flat panel monitor of high quality color; and my mouse makes many actions simply point and click. The printer is a color printer with scanner capable of reading print as well as color photographs. This system cost $1,000.

The same story could be repeated for the cost of many products, although some prices have gone up. With an undefined unit for our money driven by the short-time money profit motive, prices go up. Inflation is caused by the ambiguity of the money unit. Since no one knows the denominational meaning of "dollar" everyone defends himself or herself by expecting the money they receive each year to increase—that is inflation.

GDP is the total price we pay for what we produce. It should be called the Gross Domestic Price instead of the Gross Domestic Product. Understood as price, we should expect it to go down, not up. If we were a new country as we were 200 years ago, we should expect the GDP to go up. Everything needed to be built: new roads, factories, boats, trucks, railroads, schools, and houses. However, once built, their costs decline as they only require maintenance, so the GDP should have peaked and begun to decline. Instead, our GDP has continued to explode, depleting our resources and polluting our environment.

In an already rich country, a rising GDP is a sign of cancer. In a poor country, a rising GDP should mean that hungry people are getting more food, that housing is improving, and that schools are being built. But in a rich country, a rising GDP probably means waste and pollution. Once a certain level of wealth is reached, the GDP should stop growing and should start declining, although the quality of life should continue to improve.

For example, in the year that a new house is built the entire price of the house is added to the GDP. Thereafter, the house needs only to be maintained. The best materials and design would mean minimum maintenance. In the year after construction, then, that house should add nothing to the GDP.

Considering the impact of just that house, the GDP would be lower than the previous year. Multiply that example to the millions of homes and other commodities that add to the GDP in the year of their production. Once produced those commodities would cause the GDP to be lower in subsequent years. The better the commodities are built and maintained, the lower the GDP in subsequent years.

We live in a time when we expect the GDP to rise every year. At the same time we lament air pollution and resource depletion. We worry about running out of places to put our trash, and we fear that existing landfills will pollute our underground water. We can repair the problem by recycling, but that will not be enough. We must also remodel by learning to expect the GDP to go down and to celebrate when it does.

A second thing we should expect with each annual review of GDP/Hours is for hours worked to decrease. If we are producing high quality products that require minimum maintenance, we should expect to work less and have more free time each year.

Chapter 16
Maintaining Full Employment

Our present mode of economic thinking has us trying to solve the problem of unemployment by small repairs. The present mode of thinking has us looking for ways to create more jobs. Creating more jobs takes us in the wrong direction. We should be seeking ways to reduce work, not increase it. At the same time, everyone should have a job. Full employment should be as much a national priority as reducing work.

To short-time economics, striving for full employment while reducing work is an absurd contradiction in terms, somewhat like the idea of an automobile. A vehicle that could propel itself must have seemed a contradiction in terms to people in the time of horse drawn carriages.

In lifetime economics, there is a simple and effective way to achieve full employment while increasing free time, namely, to reduce standard work time by the rate of unemployment, whether it is the workday, the workweek, or the workyear.

In 1960, the workweek for non-farm workers was 38.6 hours. By 2001 it was down to 34.2. This is what we should expect to happen. Unemployment in 2001 was 4.8 percent of the labor force. Therefore, to move closer to full employment we should have reduced the average workweek in 2002 by 4.8 percent to 32.6 hours. That's a four-day workweek.

Some unemployment might remain because people would discover that they could do the same work in less time, so no new hires would occur. If that happened, then the workweek should again be reduced by the rate of unemployment. By this process, we would wring out the unnecessary work time—the running grinders without touching the work.

What would reducing the workweek do to wages and prices? Emotionally, we all want the numbers on our paycheck to get larger. However, we saw that the numbers on our paychecks went up from 1960 to 2001 while their purchasing power dropped. With undefined money, the numbers are misleading. The real price is what matters. The real price is work time. If work time goes down, we have realized real profit. With the workweek becoming shorter, we have a gain that is priceless, more free time to enjoy life.

Reducing the workweek by 4.8 percent should reduce pay by 4.8 percent. Should we object to such a reduction? We should if we want to stay in the repair mode of working longer hours for pay increases that are consumed by inflation. If we want the new model of less work with a simultaneously rising living standard, then we should welcome work time and pay reductions. That reduction would only seem bad because other changes would accompany the reduction that would increase the purchasing power of our paychecks.

Who now pays to maintain the unemployed? People who are working pay to maintain the unemployed. Reducing the workweek and reducing our pay merely lets the unemployed do the work and earn the money that we now give for their support anyway.

The unemployed also raise other costs for us. If they are related to us, we may find them living on our sofa. If they are strangers, we may find them becoming predators, thieves making their living by robbing our cars and homes. Or they may become homeless and embarrass us by their sight and pleas for money.

Unemployed people also become unhealthy. When they get sick they go to emergency rooms whose cost is passed on to the employed. Had they been employed, they might never have contracted the illness and that would have saved us the cost.

What happens to the children of the unemployed? They lack positive role models. They lack hope. They may become lifelong burdens on the employed. In short, there are now many hidden costs to working long hours instead of letting other people share the work by reducing the time and money that we spend on the job. If those costs were taken into account, the reductions in work time would be real while the reductions in pay would be more than offset by the reduced burden of paying to maintain the unemployed.

Under the present system, you do the work and give the pay through taxes to the unemployed. Under the system I am proposing, you get more free time and lower taxes while the presently unemployed become employed and do the work to pay their own way.

With full employment, we can expect many costs to decrease including the costs of welfare, medical care, police, the courts, and prison. Nothing does more for high self-esteem, good health, and good behavior than a good job.

Chapter 17

Saving Time: Free Time as a National Priority

I am a retired university professor. I taught sociology at the university level for 37 years, 2 years at Ohio State University and 35 years at Southern Illinois University Edwardsville. I continue to teach part time. I love my job. I wrote the first draft of this book in 1997 because I was on sabbatical.

Sabbatical gets its name from the Sabbath, the day of rest. Faculty members are eligible to apply for a sabbatical every seven years. We write a proposal that is reviewed by a series of university officials. If they judge the proposal worthy, they approve the sabbatical. My sabbatical was for one semester, 16 weeks. During that time I had no classes to teach so I could devote my time to study and writing.

I wrote the draft of this book on my fourth sabbatical. During my first one I wrote a general theory of cooperation. Part of it is what you read here in the chapter about language, writing, numbers, and money as media of communication. That theory was published in the *International Journal of Comparative Sociology* in 1985.

During my second sabbatical I studied cooperatives. I traveled around the country learning that cooperatives are very popular among farmers and that many corporations are cooperatives. I met people in food co-ops, and I learned about the great success of the Mondragon Cooperatives in the Basque area of Spain. Their rules limit the amount paid to their top executives to no more than three times the amount paid to their lowest paid members, and the system works wonderfully well.

The basic principle that rules cooperatives is share the profit with the people who produced it. For example, farmers own grain elevators cooperatively so that whatever profit the elevators make is returned to the farmers as dividends. In food co-ops, profits are distributed to member customers according to their patronage. The more they spend at the co-op, the larger their share of profit. The success of the sharing principle of cooperatives influenced my thinking presented in this book.

During my third sabbatical I studied currency exchange rates. The results of that research have been published in the *Applied Behavioral Science Review* and appear in this book.

During the sabbatical when I wrote this book, I completed work on world population growth. After this book, I studied correlates of national wealth and converted the results to a computer simulation. So you can say that ideas in this book are the result of these sabbaticals. Had I not had them, my teaching duties would have left me without the free time I needed to develop these ideas.

The university encouraged faculty like me to take early retirement, but I did not want to retire. Because I spend my time teaching, reading, and writing, I am constantly learning more. I think I get better at what I do as time goes by. Instead of retiring, I wanted to teach fewer classes but keep teaching. I think of re-tiring as getting new treads—new tires. I like the interaction with young people and all the new things I learn. Computers are still new, and I like learning the things that can be done with them. So I retired but continue to teach part-time.

The benefits of my good job with periodic sabbaticals make me want people in other jobs to have similar benefits. I would like to see more free time become a national priority. Everyone should have the opportunity for sabbaticals. The traditional pattern for many people is to work five days a week for 50 weeks a year, have a two-week vacation (hardly time enough to start a vacation), and work until retirement at age 65. That is a wartime schedule. Life is too precious and production methods are too advanced to work that intensely. It is time to free that most precious resource, life time.

I see the annual review leading to more free time for the entire labor force. It pains me to see others leave home at 6:30 or 7:00 in the morning to struggle through commuter traffic to do work that could probably be made obsolete, and then to become snarled in rush hour traffic to arrive home exhausted and irritable. Often both parents work this kind of schedule, leaving their children home alone after school. It does not have to be this way. We have the means to work less time while accomplishing more at less cost.

More free time will be ours if we focus on reducing how much we produce each year by producing higher quality products in the first place and maintaining them well thereafter. This would reduce the Gross Domestic Price portion of the GDP per hour equation. It would conserve resources and reduce pollution. Then, by reducing work time by the rate of unemployment, we would have more free time to enjoy our children, our homes, our communities, and our world. One remodel that will help achieve more free time is lower taxes.

Chapter 18

A Sustainable Path to Lower Taxes

Lower taxes are the natural consequence of good government. Good government is making decisions that make future decisions less necessary. A good policy results in less need for government and less need for the services that government provides. For example, a policy of full employment at full wages (GDP per hour) would result in everyone having a good job with a paycheck that empowered them to pay for whatever they needed. This would make all the government expenditures that we call welfare unnecessary. Single parents could afford childcare. And because free time would increase for everyone, they would need less childcare. Taxes now raised to pay for welfare could be eliminated.

Unemployment and poverty wages also create taxes for police protection and prisons. Good jobs at fair wages would make those taxes unnecessary. Internationally, with all currencies exchanging at work time, all countries would experience rising standards of living and declining conflict. Consequently, military spending, now about a trillion dollars worldwide, could be lowered if not eliminated.

Tax policy should hasten the remodeling process. Today tax policy is complex because it is motivated by insecurity and hoarding. Everyone wants loopholes so they can escape taxes. Communities refuse to pass bond issues to build new schools because the higher taxes may force them to eat less or lose their homes. Good tax policy should simplify taxes in a way that makes taxation less necessary.

The flat tax proposal of recent presidential candidate Steven Forbes excited a lot of interest because of its simplicity. Instead of hundreds of special tax rules, with a flat tax everyone would pay the same percent of their income. However, Forbes' proposal was deceptive because such a tax is simple but not flat. A tax cannot be flat unless incomes are also flat. If incomes are vastly unequal, a fixed percentage rate is an unequal tax.

Incomes denominated in hours would move incomes toward equality. We would recognize that centuries of income for a year's work is unreasonable and unjustifiable. Some people might be paid multiples of what others are paid, but the multiplier would be more reasonable. Some people might be paid triple time for the special nature of their work and novices or trainees might be paid half time. In that context a flat tax would be fair and equitable.

Most, perhaps all, deductions would be unneeded and unsought. Deductions are a symptom of absurdly unequal incomes and the stress that too little income causes. If everyone were receiving incomes within a reasonable range of equality, no one would receive obscenely large incomes, which cause other people to be underpaid. People could easily accept justified income differences.

I think the most important tax rule we need is an upper limit on income. It should be a reasonable multiple of GDP per hour. Anyone exceeding that income would have to send the rest in as an excise (excess) tax. The tax form could be very simple. For example, a 32-hour workweek for 50 weeks at $45.23 per hour equals an annual income of $72,368. Suppose that Congress decided in the interest of the general welfare that no one should receive in one year more than triple that income, or $217,104. Any income above $217,104 would be tax due. What would happen?

I doubt that anyone would send in income in excess of $217,104. Why? They would quickly find ways to distribute the excess income to other people. For example, take the corporate president who today fires 4,000 people and takes a $10 million bonus. Under the $217,104 maximum income policy, that person would owe $9,782,896 in taxes. With the bonus incentive gone, that executive would probably see giving everyone a bonus as a better choice than firing them. (They changed the word to "downsizing" to make it sound more humane.) Fewer people would be unemployed and people would have more disposable income. In a corporation of 10,000 employees, $9,782,896 would give each employee a bonus of $978. Think of the economic benefits of such a bonus policy.

Ten thousand employees and their families would have an additional $978 to spend. This would translate into effective demand for needed goods. One CEO has no needs that cost $10,000,000, but 10,000 people probably have many needs they could satisfy with $978. Think of the bonus policy's impact on employee morale. Instead of seeing one overpaid executive hoard still more purchasing—and political—power, employees would see their work rewarded with a nice bonus.

Taxation is complex today because income inequality is out of control. Many incomes are too low and many are too high. Higher than needed incomes also increase political power, which causes more tax law complexities. With incomes within a reasonable range, taxation could be simple and fair as never before, not a bad remodel of taxation. A ceiling on income would encourage a wider distribution of income, which would translate into more effective demand, less need for welfare, and less need for taxes to defend against money-motivated crime.

Chapter 19

Saving Money: Why Socialism Failed

The repair mode of saving money has people depositing money into a savings account on a regular basis and collecting interest on it. The problem with this mode is that savings rarely keep up with inflation for most people. So while people think they are saving money, they are in fact losing it. Under the prevailing economic paradigm, it is better to spend your money as soon as you get it because it will never have as much purchasing power again.

In economics aimed at increasing life time, we would understand saving money in two new ways. First, we would understand that as time goes by prices move downward and the value of money increases. Therefore, if we put money in the bank today, tomorrow it will have more purchasing power. We won't need interest to deceive us into thinking that our money is growing when in fact it is losing value. The money deposited today will gain in purchasing power because the cost of things generally will decline as securely employed people work more effectively and efficiently.

The second sense in which we will understand saving money in the remodel paradigm is as the main means by which we realize personal freedom of choice. It is important to save money as an institution, as an instrument for making decisions and choices. The danger with economics today is that people on the losing side of transactions seek ways to avoid using money at all. Groups try to get by with barter or by withdrawing from the larger society into small enclaves. We need people to have confidence in money as a way of regulating our relationships with each other. We need to understand that it is money that gives us freedom and that abandoning its use is not a wise way to cope with money mischief.

In general, there are three ways to regulate cooperation. The first is exemplified by life in a family. Life in a family is regulated by the intimate knowledge members have of each other. In a family, everyone knows everyone else. Rights and responsibilities are distributed and guaranteed by everyone's knowledge of each other. Fathers, mothers, sons and daughters, sisters and brothers, these terms suggest some of the traditional rights and responsibilities of family members. Family life is kept organized by familiarity.

Familiarity works only on a small scale. As a group enlarges and more and more people become involved, there are bound to be strangers included. Then another method of organizing rights and responsibilities is needed, namely, bureaucracy, which is another form of government.

Bureaucracy is organization by written rules and regulations. In a bureaucracy, rights and duties are expressed in job descriptions and memos. The chain of command is written on the organization chart. People send and receive memos explaining what they are expected to do. At frequent meetings, people decide what to do.

Bureaucracy supports cooperation on a larger scale than the family because it enables people who are strangers to coordinate their work. However, bureaucracy also reaches an upper limit of scale. Bureaucracies specialize. They produce certain products and not others. An automobile company has no farms or clothing stores. Yet its employees need food and clothing.

Bureaucracy overcomes its limitations by paying employees money. With money, employees can shop for their own groceries and clothing, and the bureaucracy can concentrate on what it specializes in producing.

Money transcends the limits of family and the limits of bureaucracy. Money is the mode for organizing cooperation on the largest scale. People can receive and spend money far beyond the boundaries of their families and their bureaucratic places of work. Money gives them the freedom to choose where they want to work, where they want to live, what they want to eat, and what they want to wear. Money is the quintessential means of personal freedom and choice.

Money today gets blamed for problems it does not cause. For example, people sometimes say that money causes greed. The implication is that if we abolished money we would do away with greed. Unfortunately, if we abolished money, our standard of living would plummet and we would lose a great amount of personal choice.

Socialism failed because socialists tried to reduce the boundaries where money could govern relationships. They misdiagnosed the problem as private ownership of the means of production when the true problem was ambiguity of the money unit. The people who supported socialism saw private ownership of the means of production as the problem. They thought that government ownership would take power away from the few owners of the means of production and restore it to the many people.

Government ownership reduces the role of money. Private ownership increases the role of money. Private ownership ruled by money lets owners buy and sell what they own when they want. Money makes such sales possible. Money gives people freedom to buy and sell at will. In place of money, socialists thought that they could rely on democracy. They claimed that a socialist government would decide things democratically.

When they tried to replace private ownership with government ownership and democracy, socialists discovered that making decisions democratically was very difficult. The channels of communication quickly became congested. Imagine the difficulty of deciding everything by voting. To solve the congestion problem, two things happened. First, a few individuals emerged as leaders to make the needed decisions. This was oligarchy and explains why so many socialist systems are identified with a single person, Lenin in the Soviet Union, Mao Tse Tung in China, and Fidel Castro in Cuba. Second, socialist countries were hard on dissenters. Dissent is difficult to process democratically. Therefore, dissenters were often viewed as troublemakers.

With the decline of socialism after the disintegration of the Soviet Union, many people are searching for a solution to the excessive concentration of wealth that occurs in a capitalist system such as in the United States. In the U.S., money and the political power that comes with it have become more concentrated than ever. CEOs fire thousands of employees and then give themselves big bonuses. The stock market explodes upward while taxes and debt follow suit.

The solution to the problem that socialism sought to solve with government ownership is a clear and appropriate definition of the money denominator. With the correct unit for that most important instrument of modern life, money, we can have the economic justice that socialists want with the economic freedom that capitalists want. While we can expect some income inequality with wages negotiated in terms of GDP per hour, because people would negotiate in terms of clocks and calendars, we can expect the range of variation to be a small fraction of what it is now.

Chapter 20

Beyond Capitalism: Autonomy

The model being repaired today, which I have been calling short-time economics, is also called capitalism. It stands for accumulation of money and power in the hands of whoever is the most competitive and selfish. It assumes a world of scarcity and encourages people to hoard whatever is valuable, including the means of production and distribution. Capitalism encourages people to hoard their jobs. All this hoarding produces glut and gluttony for some people and scarcity and hunger for others. Though it claims to be the source of abundance, which it is for some, it causes scarcity for others.

Capitalism perverts meanings. Although a little reflection shows that cooperation promotes the best relationships, capitalism says that the best relationships are competitive. We are told that the New World Order requires that we become more competitive. Would it not be better if we became more cooperative? Under capitalist labels, employees are not fired, companies are downsized. Agreements that allow companies to export jobs to low wages countries are called Free Trade Agreements, such as the North American Free Trade Agreement. Nothing is said of fair trade because that would be unprofitable.

From a cooperative perspective the world looks very different. The earth is beautiful and bountiful, a place that has sufficient resources for everyone to live well if we live wisely. Cooperation, not competition, is the means to wealth. In this model, it is best to cooperate. It says: Look for ways to cooperate with your neighbors. Internationally, we want all people in all countries to live wisely and well. A cooperative attitude encourages countries to produce what they need locally, not to give their people jobs, because we would want all people to have more free time, but to conserve resources. Transporting goods around the world wastes energy and pollutes the air and water.

A lot of energy is wasted transporting things from one part of the world to another. Ravi Batra, in *The Myth of Free Trade* (1993), estimates that as much as 25 percent of the energy used to transport goods traded internationally could be saved if the goods were made at home. We add to pollution when one company ships goods X from point A to point B while another company ships goods X from point B to point A. Why do they do it? Because they are in competition and it is illegal to tell each other what they are doing. In the new model of lifetime economics, it is good economics for everyone to save time and money by telling each other what they are shipping and where.

The appeal of capitalism is freedom. It's too bad that freedom for one person comes by reducing someone else's freedom. Genuine freedom comes when everyone is free, when my actions increase your freedom as well as my own. Freedom comes when our basic needs are fully met. Freedom comes when each of us has control over our own life without reducing anyone else's control over theirs.

Under capitalism, we have the best government money can buy. The hoarders make the biggest contributions to political campaigns either openly or behind closed doors.

In lifetime economics, politics is more democratic because money is distributed more equitably. If economist Paul Samuelson is right and money is like votes, we cannot have democracy if most of the votes are in the hands of a minority. A country can be democratic only to the degree that income is distributed equitably, a word close in meaning to equally.

For these reasons, I like to think of this new model as beyond capitalist zero-sum freedom to personal autonomy for everyone.

The word "autonomy" comes from two Greek words: *auto*, meaning self, and *nomos*, meaning management. A person who is autonomous controls his or her own life. They have personal power. Parents look forward to the day that their children become autonomous. That's what growing up is about.

Autonomous people are also good cooperators. They are quick to identify what needs to be done and eager to get it done. They are easy and fun to work with. When everyone is autonomous, we will be living in the remodeled economy. Cooperation: The Wealth of Nations Game simulates autonomy as explained in the last chapter.

Chapter 21
Paying Debt on Time

Debt today is exploding by a mathematical imperative. Debt will continue to explode until we change the math.

The mathematical imperative is known as compound interest. Albert Einstein said that compound interest is as dangerous as an atomic bomb. His reason was that they grow by similar mathematical formulae.

$$\text{Sum} = \text{Amount} (1 + r)^{\text{Time}}$$

$$\text{Energy} = \text{Mass} (\text{Velocity of Light})^2$$

An amount of money, $100, at an interest rate, r, say 6 percent, after 1 year's time becomes the sum $106. After two year's time it becomes $112.36 as interest on interest begins to take hold. Like a snowball rolling downhill, the sum grows ever more rapidly. Unlike a snowball, which will eventually reach the bottom of the hill, compound interest has no mathematical limit.

Compound interest is used as an incentive to save or to buy insurance. As an incentive to save, we are shown how compound interest will make a small deposit grow until it's a fortune. As an incentive to buy insurance, we are shown how compound interest will make our premium payments grow to huge cash values.

The problem ignored is the source of the growth or, more correctly, who pays the growth. Money does not grow like corn or wheat. The growing sum is a growing obligation on someone else to pay. For example, as a savings account grows, the bank that has that account has a growing obligation to the owner of that account. How is the bank going to meet that obligation? It must find people to whom to make loans. Those loans are necessary to obtain the interest money to match the growing savings account. A growing savings account always has its counterpart in a growing debt. For savings to grow by compound interest, debts must grow by compound interest as well.

A similar situation occurs with insurance. As the cash value of policies increases, the insurance company must find ways to obtain additional income to meet its growing obligation to policyholders. This would not be an insurmountable problem if the mathematics matched the nature of economic reality. However, compound interest is "thermonuclear" and economies are not.

Driven by the mathematical imperative of thermonuclear compounding interest, all forms of debt, home mortgage debt, consumer credit card debt, farm debt, corporate debt, local, state, and federal government debt, and the debts of Third World countries to First World banks, have exploded beyond the capacity of debtors to pay.

Consider federal debt. It is so large and growing so fast that it is impossible to say how large it is without immediately understating it. Let's fix it for the moment at $6 trillion. As with millions and billions of dollars, trillions of dollars are hard to comprehend in real terms, so let's convert the debt to work time at the 2001 GDP per hour rate of $45.23.

$$\frac{\$6,000,000,000,000}{\$45.23}$$

132,655,317,267 hours of work

At 32 hours a workweek for 50 weeks, one person works 1600 hours in a year. Therefore, 132,655,317,267 hours of work equals 82,909,573 years of work, that is, a year's work of 82,909,573 people. Given the 2001 U.S. employed labor force of 135 million people, the federal debt is equal to 61 percent of the entire production of the labor force in a year.

Before we can think about how to pay this debt, we need to see the total as a slice in time of an exponential process. This is a snapshot of one moment in an explosion. If the process could be stopped where it is now, then paying the debt would require transferring the equivalent of 61 percent of the total production of the nation for one year to the debt holders.

This year, 2003, the federal government is facing a deficit nearing $500 billion. Federal debt is projected to increase by 4 or 5 trillion dollars in the next few years. If the federal debt grows to $10 trillion, which it is very likely to do, consider what compound interest will add to it in a single year. Six percent of $10 trillion is $600 billion. That is added interest in one year.

So what can be done about federal debt?

Absolutely the first thing that must be done is to change the arithmetic. There is no way to pay the debt if interest continues to compound. Leave the compound interest formula in place and the people of the United States shall owe their creditors some incredible amount, like many times more than everything ever produced on earth.

There are many formulae for reckoning interest more realistically than a rate that compounds, for example, simple interest. Simple interest is interest only on the principal sum borrowed, no interest on the interest. Compounding occurs because interest accrues on interest. So Congress could rule that we owe only principal plus simple interest. There are two difficulties with this solution.

First, it requires separating principal from interest when the debt all looks the same. The debt we have today, it can be argued, is the original debt in 1790 increased by compounding interest over 213 years. In that sense, it's all interest. The original debt of $75 million in 1790 was itself the Revolutionary War debt of about $40 million increased by compound interest from the end of the war until 1790. By the simple interest argument, on the original $40 million in principal at six percent interest we would owe $2.4 million per year for 220 years (1783 to 2003) for a total of $568 million. That's millions, not billions.

The second problem is that holders of the debt now are not the original holders. From the point of view of recent buyers, the money they paid to buy the debt certificates was principal even though it may have been the result of compounding interest. How can we be fair to them?

I have come to the conclusion that the only realistic way to begin to solve the debt problem is to stop adding interest to principal. Money is simply a bookkeeping tool. As such it should be paid for as any other tool, namely, by a fee to the bookkeeper for his or her work time.

Interest has been destructive as long as and wherever it has been used. The world's religions attest to that. Judaism, Christianity, and Islam all condemn interest. Why? Because they record the damage interest has done. If interest were abolished in all its forms everywhere, we could pay our just debts, whether they are the debts of the federal government, our state and local governments, our credit card debts, farm debts, or mortgage debts. Otherwise, there is no earthly way these debts will be paid. A few debtors escape, only temporarily and only by burdening someone else with a still larger debt.

We must change the charge for borrowing money from a rate to a service fee. Once interest is changed from a rate to a fee for work done, debts of all kinds could begin to be paid off. It would stop the growth of federal debt in its tracks. Federal deficits each year are very close to the amount owed in interest. Then Congress could schedule payment of the debt by reasonable installments over a period of years. Households could pay their mortgages in half the time and use the money saved to pay for such important things as home maintenance and education for their children. Farmers could pay off their debts. And the biggest debtors of all, the corporations, could begin to pay off their debts.

The abolition of interest would save enormous amounts of money and lower taxes dramatically. Can it be done? It certainly can. The biggest obstacle is shortsighted, narrow self-interest. We all ask, "How will this affect me?" Many people depend on interest for their income. Pensions are based on interest income, including my own.

It's a remodeling problem. We cannot simply repair the problem, for example, by reducing interest rates. A lower interest rate leaves compounding in place; it merely slows it down. And a lower interest rate reduces the income of people whose income and livelihood depends on interest. Something more basic must be done. We cannot continue to use exponential arithmetic and expect anything other than exponential growth in claims by creditors and obligations of debtors. Math does not yield to politics. To solve the debt problem, the mathematics must be changed. I offer you the remodeling idea of using a fee for service instead of the exponential arithmetic of interest rates.

For example, when a family borrowed from a bank to buy a home, the bank would distribute the loan payments over a period of years, as it does now except that the amount would be only principal. A $100,000 loan, if repaid over 20 years, would mean 240 monthly payments of $466.67. The bank would add a small bookkeeping fee to each payment to cover the work done by bank employees recording the transaction.

The abolition of interest rates would mean that people who put money into a savings account would not collect interest on it. Nothing would be lost and much would be gained. Banks would no longer be in danger of going bankrupt because they would no longer be required to seek out more and more debtors to cover their growing obligation to savers. The gain would come as the general price level declined with growing worker effectiveness and efficiency. So the longer people left money in the bank, the more purchasing power it would gain.

There would also be an incentive to pay debts as quickly as possible. For example, a family would want to pay its home mortgage in 10 or 15 years instead of 20 or 25 years because the payment would represent more purchasing power the longer they waited to pay it off. Better to pay off the mortgage in current money than to wait to pay with money earned in future years that would have more purchasing power.

Doesn't that jar your mind a bit? We usually think of money as losing value in the future so we should spend it right away. Here I am saying pay your mortgage right away because money will buy more in the future.

It's not the same money. Under a system where goods are improving in quality and work time and prices are going down, the money I earn today buys less today than the money I will earn ten years from now. Why wait to pay the mortgage with future money that has more purchasing power? Use the money with less purchasing power today to pay the mortgage. Saving is another matter. If I can save the money, good. It will gain purchasing power over time.

Time is additive, not exponential. The economy is organized on time. Work is scheduled by the day and hour, entry into the labor force and retirement are schedule by age. Rent, mortgage payments, utility payments, credit card payments, and taxes are collected monthly and yearly. The clock and the calendar operate by addition. We add time and add days. We can multiply time and days, but it makes no sense to raise time to an exponential power. It's mathematical nonsense to raise an hour to a power, for example, 2 hours squared or cubed. We need to treat interest as mathematically inappropriate and stop it.

But that leaves the question, how are people living on interest to be supported? How are retired persons like myself to be supported? Here we need to remodel Social Security.

Chapter 22
Social Security

The idea behind social security is a sound one. Working people set aside a portion of their earnings as savings during their working years, and then are supported by those savings in their retirement. By putting the savings into a common pool, the savings are available also as an insurance fund to cover such needs as disability and death. It is "social" because many people are forming a common trust fund to share their risks. It is "security" because ultimately, in the final analysis, our only real security is in each other. The principle is the same as that used by insurance companies and the banks, most notably, the Federal Reserve System.

To overcome the problem of people losing confidence in banks and withdrawing their money only to find that banks did not have enough cash to satisfy everyone's claims (bank loans are based on checking account deposits), which would precipitate bankruptcies, the banks joined together to pool their cash so that it could be quickly transferred to where a run on a bank was occurring. With the extra cash, a bank could reassure depositors that their money was safe. An insurance fund works the same way in getting funds to where they are needed, as was the intention of the Social Security Administration.

My grandmother lived on social security from the time she turned 65 until her death shortly after her 100th birthday. For 35 years she received a check that supported her modestly but comfortably most of that time. She turned 65 in 1950. Social security payments were small but prices were also low. Inflation, however, reduced the purchasing power of those payments. My grandmother was frugal and managed her money well. Today, though, you and I know that Social Security is in trouble.

The problem, as always, is defining the problem. What is the problem? Is it that the baby boomer generation is coming along when retirees will outnumber workers? Is it continuing inflation? Is it federal deficits that are being covered by transfers of Social Security funds into general federal funds? From my viewpoint, these are symptoms, not the real problem. At this point, having read this much, you should be thinking that I am going to say that the problem is that money needs to be defined in terms of work time. If so, you are correct.

Time is the most important measure we have. We measure our lives with time. What is the most important date in the year for each of us? Our birthday. Consider how important age is to each of us. We organize our lives by time. Social Security needs to be organized by time also. If we stabilize money by defining its value in hours of work, we can build a sound social security system.

I think of the new model of social security as Simple Security. During our working years we should set aside a portion of our pay in a common fund with everyone else. We would then draw on that fund during periods of illness and disability, retirement and death. The power of money defined in time is that the arithmetic for deciding how much to save becomes clear. No more ambiguity about how much a dollar is worth and, therefore, ambiguity about how many dollars we need to save in order to have enough dollars when we need them.

Here I will give you a model of how Simple Security might be set up. The idea is to set up a lifetime budget. Start with a reasonable estimate of how long people can expect to live. I will use 100 years. Average life expectancy will probably always be less than 100 years, so we would have a cushion built in for unforeseen costs.

Next, we would estimate the cost of a comfortable standard of living during different periods of a lifetime. I say during different periods of a lifetime because needs are different at different times. For example, a couple with young children may need more than a retired couple. With prices expressed in work time, it should be possible to add up all the costs of food, clothing, housing, education, communication, and travel in the real terms of how much time a person needs to work to meet those needs. There are many people with the information and skills to do this kind of planning in a professional and accurate way.

Then we would estimate how many hours over the years people need to work to pay living expenses during these various periods. Say, for example, that they want to have sufficient income for 40 years of retirement. We would not need to assume that retirement comes only at 65 when work life is over. We could retire for a month or two each year. The figure of 40 years is meant to suggest a lifetime total of years not working.

Given the information, by simple arithmetic, we could know how much we needed to save in work hours worth of money. We could also know how many work hours worth of money we needed to pay for goods and services needed while still working.

This entire scenario of Simple Security depends on doing a lot of other remodeling as well. For example, an upper limit on income has to be put in place. We cannot have millionaires and billionaires hoarding work hours worth of money and expect the arithmetic of Simple Security to work out.

Chapter 23

Cap the Top!

The most important and beneficial action we can take is to set an upper limit to income. There are natural limits to how much food people can eat, to how much clothing people can comfortably wear, to how much work people can naturally do, to how fast cars can travel safely, and to how high planes can fly in the atmosphere.

There are no natural limits to how much money people can accumulate. As numbers with no physically known quantity to define their value, money numbers can grow to infinity. Senator Everett Dirksen of Illinois used to say, "A billion here, a billion there, and pretty soon you're talking about a lot of money."

In 1995 the richest 400 people in the United States held assets equal to $1 billion each. Only four years later, they held assets equal to $2 billion *each*. Recently, the director of the New York Stock Exchange claimed payment of $140 million dollars. Lottery winnings routinely exceed tens of millions of dollars. These are signs that money is exploding out of control. We must cap the top.

On September 25, 1999, *The Kansas City Star*, reported on the health of the U.S. household as follows.

It's not trickle down; it's gush up.

Over the 10 years between 1989 and 1999, the 400 richest Americans gained an average of $1.6 billion in wealth. In that time, the net worth of the median U.S. household went down $4,700.

It would take less than 5 percent of the wealth of the richest 400, $48.4 billion, to lift all Americans above the poverty line.

The minimum wealth to be on the 400 list—
$125 million—would take a minimum wage
earner 11,669 (12,000) years to earn.

The 400 richest individuals own as many assets
as 50 million American households.

The top 1 percent now has more than the
bottom 95 percent.

Income must be limited. It would be shameful for one or
two members of a household to hoard all of its resources. So we
should not allow members of the larger household to hoard
billions of dollars while other members struggle to stay alive.

I will cite two persons who supported limited income. In
1872 philosopher John Ruskin (1819-1900), who himself grew
up in a wealthy family, wrote,

> I have long been convinced that there should be
> an upper limit to the income and property of the
> upper classes. The temptation to use every energy
> in the accumulation of wealth being thus removed,
> another and a higher ideal of the duties of
> advanced life would be necessarily created in the
> national mind; by withdrawal of those who had
> attained the prescribed limits of wealth from
> commercial competition, earlier worldly success
> and earlier marriage with all its beneficent moral
> results would become possible to the young; while
> the older men of active intellect, whose sagacity is
> now lost or warped in the furtherance of their own
> meanest interest, would be induced unselfishly to
> occupy themselves in the superintendence of
> public institutions, or furtherance of public
> advantage[1].

---

1 The Works of John Ruskin, Volume V. Time and Tide. England,

Imagine how much more positively the affairs of Enron might have gone if its executives had been limited to a reasonable income.

The other person I will mention who supported limiting income is United States Senator Huey Long (1893 - 1935). In his 1933 book, *Every Man a King*, Long proposed eliminating poverty by limiting income to $5 million dollars a year and giving every family a minimum income of $5000 per year and old-age pensions of $30 per month to elderly people who had less than $10,000 in cash. Many people supported Long's Share the Wealth program, including many U.S. Senators. He wrote his story of what would happen if he were elected President in his 1935 book *My First Days in the White House*. You can read the book on the Internet. On September 10, 1935, Long was assassinated.

Where should the limit be set?

Whatever the limit, I think it should be set on some principle. For example, one principle might be that no one should receive more income than they can spend in a lifetime. Note the word is spend, not invest. There is probably no limit to how much a person can invest in a lifetime. There is a limit to how much a person can spend for food, clothing, housing, vacations, medical care, education, and such personal needs and wants.

Another principle could be that the highest income should be no more than 10 times the income of the lowest. If the lowest income is $10,000 a year, the highest would be $100,000. This principle would keep income in relative alignment.

Whatever the principle, a general fact is that the lower the upper limit is set, the wider the benefits of production will be spread. For example, if the limit is set at $1 billion, the benefit will be limited to what is today income in excess of $1 billion,

Smith and Elder, 1872:11.

not as much as the excess above, say, $1 million. The lower the upper limit, the more people with lower incomes will benefit from increased incomes.

Chapter 24

A Peace Agenda

The 20th Century has been a century of war. In the new millennium, there continues to be dozens of wars around the world. When a crisis occurs, we rush planes, missiles, guns, and troops to the spot. We seem not to know how to make peace. American troops are trained to kill; they are not trained to build institutions. We are hard pressed to say what the tools of peace are. In this chapter, I reiterate many earlier ideas in the form of a peace agenda. This peace agenda states four principles that promote peace rather than war. If we enter crisis situations with these principles in mind, I believe that the outcome is more likely to be healthy rather than harmful to all concerned.

1. TOOLS, NOT WEAPONS

When facing a crisis, let us ask ourselves what tools would help meet people's needs instead of striking people with weapons. Weapons always waste. If they are used, they waste. If they are not used, they waste. At a time when as many as a billion men, women, and children in the world live in acute poverty without food or clean water, a trillion dollars a year is spent on weapons whose only purpose is to kill people and destroy property. A trillion dollars is a million million, $1,000,000,000,000. Imagine how people's needs could be better met if a fraction of the effort represented by that money

Gift to the United Nations from the Soviet Union in 1959

were devoted to tools instead of weapons.

On April 18, 1953, President Dwight David Eisenhower said,

> Every gun that is made, every warship launched, every rocket fired signifies, in the final sense, a theft from those who hunger and are not fed, those who are cold and are not clothed. This world in arms is not spending money alone. It is spending the sweat of its laborers, the genius of its scientists, the hopes of its children.

History will judge us as fools for wasting so much for so little. Weapons have never made peace. Tools make peace. We must lead with tools, not tanks. The only gain in weapons manufacture is paper profits to the manufacturers. Spending on weapons is driven by these pseudo-profits and the dependence of families on income from weapons factories. We need to employ the people currently in war industries in peace industries, namely, toolmaking.

We need to convert this waste as soon as possible to the production of wealth. Congress must be lobbied to appropriate the monies now being wasted on weapons we don't need and should not use for rebuilding our roads, bridges, water systems, schools, houses and factories. It is time to beat our swords into plowshares, tools that meet people's needs. Our foreign policy must be shifted from selling weapons worldwide to selling tools. The longer we delay the poorer and more insecure we become.

2. COOPERATION, NOT CONFLICT

Examination of history shows that human beings have lived well to the degree that we have cooperated. Cooperation makes everything easier; conflict makes everything more difficult. Look at the terrible destruction of World War I and World War II, millions of people killed, millions more injured, cities, roads and bridges destroyed, treasures accumulated over thousands of years destroyed in moments.

Recall the hateful stereotypes propagated by all sides in the conflict. We always demonize our enemies, only to realize eventually that they are more like us than not and that we are part of the same race, the human race. We must see beyond our self-made stereotypes to our common humanity. Our own survival depends on it. As President Kennedy said, "Mankind must put an end to war, or war will put an end to mankind."

Consider how hateful our image of the Soviet Union and its leaders was. President Ronald Reagan called it the Evil Empire. Then he met Mikhail Gorbachev and liked him. Soon thereafter, almost overnight, our attitude changed. Earlier a similar change happened with China. President Richard Nixon, the great fighter of Communism, made peace with the Chinese and today they are our biggest trading partners. Today, President George Bush has called Iraq, Iran, and North Korea the Axis of Evil. That will do no good, as such stereotypes have never done any good.

When we face a crisis, we need to ask what we can do to help both sides meet their needs. We need to harmonize rather than demonize. Not only because it's right, but also because it is in our own best lifetime interest.

3. EQUALITY, NOT INEQUALITY

The evidence of history and a comparison of contemporary countries show that countries that promote equality are more prosperous than countries that promote inequality. Equality is the cause and consequence of prosperity and justice; inequality is the cause and consequence of poverty and rebellion.

Democracy is based on the equality principle of one-person, one-vote. When first used by the Greeks, it meant rule by the mob, demon-cracy. Only gradually was the franchise extended to the general adult population and to women in the United States only in 1923. Today democracy symbolizes what most people regard as good government.

The principle of democratic political equality needs to be extended to our economy. We must institute and follow policies that share the work and that share the wealth among the largest number of people. Economic equality will optimize supply and demand. On the other hand, the growing inequality today is reducing supply and demand. That it will not be easy is evident in the defeat of the Equal Rights Amendment that simply said that no person would be discriminated against on the basis of sex, but it must be done.

4. ECONOMY, NOT WASTE

The basic economic problem that we face today is not scarcity; it is waste, the waste of materials, effort, and people in under-education, under-employment, and over-work. For a healthy and efficient economy, everyone must be educated to the limit of their ability and employed in jobs that produce real wealth, permit mobility, and maximize leisure, in short, jobs that produce the most wealth with the least work.

The aim of the peace agenda is to promote health, wealth, and wisdom worldwide. It boils down to offering all people of all ages and of all lands the hand of help rather than harm in a spirit of mutual respect and equality that we may all prosper together.

After all, as it says in the song *It's a Small World*:
  It's a world of laughter, a world of tears.
  It's a world of hopes; it's a world of fears.
  It's so much that we share that it's time you're aware
  It's a small world after all.
  [Chorus]
  It's a small world after all
  It's a small world after all
  It's a small world after all
  It's a small, small world.
  There is just one moon and one golden sun

And a smile means friendship to everyone.
Though the mountains be high and the oceans are wide
It's a small world after all.

Chapter 25

Lifetime Economics

In this chapter I bring together the ideas presented in earlier chapters that add up to what I call "Lifetime Economics." I like that name because it is economics that can be practiced our entire lifetime and because the standard of good choices that it uses is lifetime.

Rule 1: Value goods and services in lifetime.

Lifetime is the time that something is useful. Classical economists called it use time. Something has a lifetime as long as it can be used. Something that is good is better the longer it lasts. When we make something, lifetime economics says make it useful for a long time. In a word, make it durable. High quality is better than low quality. A friend of mine once pointed out that it is unwise to buy cheap flashlights. In no time they break down, and then become plastic trash. It is better to buy a high quality flashlight that will give good service for a long time. That's what the first rule of lifetime economics means.

Rule 2. Price goods and services in work time.

The more work required to produce something, the more it really costs. Therefore, it should sell at a higher price than something produced with less work. When something has a high price, we should look for an equivalent of the same quality at a lower price. That's smart shopping.

We want to reward quality workmanship that is efficient. So we should buy the products of efficient workers, which properly priced will be cheaper than the products of inefficient workers. Those who produce at higher prices will then have a reason to increase their efficiency. Efficiency should be rewarded by purchase. If the inefficient want to sell their goods, they need to become more efficient so that their products will be more affordable.

Rule 3. Maximize Profit.

In lifetime economics, profit is the difference between value and price.

$$\text{Value - Price} = \text{Profit}$$

or

$$\text{Life Time - Work Time} = \text{Free Time.}$$

When we make something well, so that it is useful for a long time, we make the most efficient use of our labor. The payoff is the free time to enjoy our wealth. That's real profit.

Short-time economics defines profit only in terms of money. Profit is the difference between the price the seller pays, labeled "cost," and the price the buyer pays: Price - Cost = Profit. In short-time economics, the goal is to buy cheap and sell dear. That is zero-sum. What the seller gains the buyer loses. Seller and buyer are competitors, if not enemies. So this idea of profit justifies the caution, buyer beware, and it explains why people are often suspicious of salespeople.

In contrast, in lifetime economics, everyone gains. As everyone produces better quality products, everyone works less and is able to enjoy life more. That's economics worthy of the name.

To maximize lifetime, 1) build things to last, and 2) service and repair regularly. To minimize work time, cooperate. To cooperate, 1) communicate, 2) specialize, and 3) reciprocate. Communicating and specializing mean sharing the work. Reciprocating means sharing the wealth.

Our capacity to cooperate develops first in our family. When the learning process is successful, we progress from egocentric infants to children who play well with others to adults who are good citizens. Michael Popkin of Active Parenting urges parents to help their children develop courage, to take known risks for a known purpose, to be responsible, to make choices and accept the consequences of those choices, and to cooperate so that they can work with others for common goals.

Beyond family, the qualities of courage, responsibility, and cooperation should be further developed in school. Along with learning reading, writing, and arithmetic, children should learn to get along with each other, to help each other, to celebrate one another's successes, and to comfort one another in failures.

This is the briefest treatment of the important role of families and schools. Much more has been written, but my focus is on the role of government and money.

Contributions of Government

Some people say that a government that governs least governs best. I say that a government that governs best governs least. The first saying puts reducing government first. It implies that no government at all would produce a wonderful world of freely cooperating individuals. I do not agree. With no government at all we might sometimes have peace and prosperity, at least on a small local scale, but at other times there would be war and chaos. We need an agency to define certain basic rules so that we know what is required of each of us in order for our actions collectively to add up to a good life for all.

The second saying, the government that governs best governs least, puts making good rules first. It means that a government that does a good job of making rules will need to do less and less as time passes. So a government that governs well will become a government that governs least. On the other hand, a government that does a bad job of making rules will find itself faced with new crises as time goes by. So a government that governs badly will find it necessary to govern more and more.

I see the essence of good government as making the right rules about money. A good government will do three things.

First, it will produce and put into circulation the correct kind of money for conducting the economic exchanges of the country. That money will be put into circulation debt-free and interest-free.

Second, the government will regulate the value of money by defining the money unit in an appropriate and objective way.

Third, the government will prevent people from hoarding money.

First, a good government will produce and put into circulation the correct kind of money debt-free and interest-free. Everyone knows that money does not grow on trees. However, how many people know where money does come from? Today, banks create more than 90 percent of our money as loans for which the banks charge interest. This system is worldwide, and it explains why debt is exploding worldwide.

Money is to an economy what blood is to the human body. The body requires a certain amount of blood that circulates without gain or loss throughout the body. If one part of the body is suddenly engorged with too much blood, the body suffers. If one part of the body loses blood, the body suffers. In a similar way, to produce a healthy economy, money must circulate throughout it, neither increasing nor decreasing as it flows.

Money created as loans by banks requires money to be removed from circulation as interest payments to the banks. This "bleeds" a portion of the economy of needed money circulation. Only people borrowing more money from the banks restores that money to circulation. In this way, to keep a constant money supply in circulation, total debt has exploded at about the rate of interest.

Bankers support this method of money creation because their assets, the counterpart of debt, explode with exploding debt. Lending at interest always makes banks richer. The richness is fragile, however, because it depends on debtors continuing to pay interest and continuing to take out larger and larger loans. Eventually, this growth exceeds everyone's ability to keep up with it and the system goes bankrupt. Bankruptcy can be postponed by creative accounting and by shifting debts to government, but bankruptcy must eventually happen because no growth process can continue without limit.

Thomas Jefferson understood the danger of having banks create money as debt requiring the payment of interest. He wrote:

> If the American people ever allow the banks to control the issuance of their currency, first by inflation and then by deflation, the banks and corporations that will grow up around them will deprive the people of all property until their children will wake up homeless on the continent their fathers occupied. The issuing power of money should be taken from the banks and restored to Congress and the people to whom it belongs. I sincerely believe the banking institutions (having the issuing power of money) are more dangerous to liberty than standing armies. My zeal against these institutions was so warm and open at the establishment of the Bank of the United States (Hamilton's foreign system) that I was derided as a maniac by the tribe of bank mongers who were seeking to filch from the public[2].

---

2 Dwinell, *The Story of Our Money*, 1946:202-3.

Too bad Jefferson is not around today. The American people have allowed the banks to control our currency throughout our history, and what Jefferson feared has happened. Debtors owe the banks far more than the total value of everything in the country. The property of the U.S. has been estimated to be worth about $8 trillion while total debt is somewhere in excess of $40 trillion and growing. If debtors gave everything to their creditors they would still owe more than they have given up. This process is not over; it continues every day.

In 1935, Gertrude Coogan published her explanation for the Great Depression in her book, *The Money Creators*. There she explained how banks increase their loans, which brings economic boon, and then contract them, forcing debtors to default their assets to the banks. Like a giant sucking machine, the banks reach out and suck in the assets of the country. In Coogan's view, the Great Depression was part of this process. It was started by banks calling in their loans. It ended when banks once again made big loans.

Government can supply the country with money in any of four ways. The first way is the best; the fourth way is the worst.

1. Government can *spend* money into circulation. It can pay people to build public facilities like roads, bridges, schools, water supply and waste treatment plants, parks and playgrounds. This is the best way for the government to put money into circulation because it gets valuable things built in the process and because the money can then circulation debt-free and interest-free.

2. Government can *lend* money into circulation. A group named Sovereignty is gathering support for this kind of government issue of money. They are asking tax-supported bodies like school boards and city, county, and state governments to endorse a petition to Congress asking for interest-free loans to tax-supported bodies for capital projects

and to pay existing debt. The plan is to have money created by the U.S. Treasury, not borrowed. With this method, the agencies receiving the money would be required to pay it back. Today these public agencies must issue bonds to finance needed public facilities. The result is that taxes are about double what they would be under the Sovereignty proposal.

For example, our school district built a new high school. To build it the district borrowed $31 million dollars by selling bonds. That loan will cost about $30 million dollars more for interest. To get one new high school we will pay taxes to support the equivalent of two high schools. If we could borrow the money interest-free from the U.S. Treasury, our tax burden would be halved. This kind of tax relief would be multiplied many-fold by adopting the Sovereignty method of government money creation nationwide. Already more than 3,000 tax bodies have endorsed the Sovereignty petition.

The Sovereignty method is good because taxpayers pay the cost of what they add to community wealth. They do not pay double the cost. This method is also good because the money is paid back. This is important if inflation is a concern.

If interest were abolished as I recommend, then borrowing could be done from local banks. Our school district would borrow the money and repay it plus a small bookkeeping fee with tax revenues. Then, instead of having to choose between library books and computers, we could equip our new high school with both.

Third, government can *issue* money. For example, Congress could mail people a check for $1,000. I cannot think of any good reason for issuing money this way. I can think of bad reasons for doing so. Today, the U.S. Congress has failed to solve the problems of unemployment and rising housing costs that are causing homelessness. The only solution it has come up with is to mail people welfare checks and food stamps. If we set prices by the standard of work time and if we reduced work time by the rate of unemployment, I believe that we would not need to give money to people by simply mailing it to them. I think that almost everyone would have gainful employment as his or her means of support.

Fourth, the worst method of money creation available to government is to *borrow* it. That is the method used worldwide almost since the invention of money. This is a terrible method because it causes debt to increase forever, at least until massive bankruptcy cripples the country. No sovereign government should ever borrow money. When it does, it loses its sovereignty to its creditors. That is why Meyer Amschel Rothschild is reputed to have said in 1790, "Let me issue and control the money supply of a nation and I care not who makes its laws."

Congress is frustrated in its efforts to balance the federal budget because the main cause is not being addressed. Cutting here and there is repair work that fails to do the job. We need to remodel, in this case, by doing what Jefferson recommended 200 years ago: have Congress issue and control the money supply of the nation. In Abraham Lincoln's words, "The privilege of creating and issuing money is not only the supreme prerogative of government, but it is the government's greatest opportunity to create abundance."

Several times I have referred to the "correct" kind of money. What is the correct kind of money? The most important thing to be correct is not the amount *of* money; it is the amount *on* money. Consider a ruler for measuring length. Which is more important, the number of rulers in circulation or the numbers on each ruler? The numbers on each ruler are more important. The number of rulers is important only in there being a ruler available when we need one. Having one ruler or two or three does not change the length of the foot. The same should be true of money. The amount of money should not change the value on money.

Government must regulate the denominator on money like it regulates the denominator on rulers. There are four ways government can regulate the denominator on money. The first one is best; the fourth one is worst.

The best way for government to regulate the money unit is to clearly define it. The unit I have proposed in this book is:

<u>Gross Domestic Price</u>
Total Hours Worked

Gross Domestic Price is now published widely, including in the *Statistical Abstract of the United States* where it is called the Gross Domestic Product. Hours worked can be calculated from Department of Labor statistics. This is the best method because the information on which it is based is clear. The calculation could be printed on the money. As people became accustomed to the Hour as the money unit, a new currency denominated in hours could replace the ones we now use. We would then have Hour Dollars. The other three methods go from bad to worst.

The second method, now the favored one, is to adjust prices according to the Consumer Price Index. Here the government has constructed a "market basket" of goods and services that is regarded as typical for an urban family of four. It then selects a base year, say 1990, and compiles the total price of that market basket of goods. That price becomes the standard. The next year the government compiles the total price of the same market basket again and compares that price with the previous year's price. If the price has gone up, there has been inflation to that degree. If the price is up 3 percent, inflation has been 3 percent. Adjustments in prices are then expected to follow that guideline.

A major problem with this method is the choice of a base year. How do we know that prices in the base year were not inflated? We don't know. So the CPI and similar indices only tell us relative prices. They cannot tell us absolute prices. Another problem is that the measure is relative to what is put into the market basket. A different set of goods and services would probably produce a different rate of inflation. However, the CPI is the best index now in use.

The third method for regulating the value of money is worse. It is interest rates. To fight rising prices, the Federal Reserve raises the interest rate. This is like fighting fire with gasoline. Raising the interest rate raises the price of everything being produced with borrowed money. Since about 98 percent of the money supply is borrowed, raising the interest rate raises the price of just about everything. Bankers would quickly stop using this method except for one thing; they make more money when they raise interest rates. They lose money when they lower interest rates. So having them in charge of controlling inflation is a conflict of interest.

The absolute worst way to regulate the value of money is to leave it to supply and demand. Orthodox economists want us to believe that the invisible hand of the market is smarter than the government. However, the market is just a name for people making decisions on the basis of their limited information, and the government is just a name for people making decisions on the basis of their limited information. It is nonsense to argue that one group is smarter than the other group.

Look at it this way. Would we let the length of rulers be decided by the supply of and demand for rulers? Certainly not. Would we let everyone decide for himself or herself if it is 8 o'clock, 9 o'clock, or 10 o'clock? Certainly not. Government defines the length of rulers and the times of day. To do otherwise would invite absolute chaos. The government is letting people negotiate the value of the dollar, and we have a lot of unnecessary chaos in our economy. That chaos has been occurring for so long that we assume it is natural. It is very unnatural. The sooner we stop it and get money properly denominated, the happier we will all be.

The third responsibility of good government is to *prevent hoarding*. The four methods for meeting this responsibility also go from best to worst. The best method is to limit income to work time. Work time is limited by the hours in the day and the capacity of the human body to work. All people share these limits. If income is limited to the amount of time people work, hoarding will be prevented.

The second method is to limit income, for example, to personal lifetime. If people could receive a total income no larger than that equivalent to working full-time for their entire lives, that would limit hoarding. For example, assuming a person could live to be 100 years old, they could earn more than 1 year of income per year but they would have to stop when their income reached 100 years' worth. This method is not as good as the first because people could hoard by getting their lifetime's worth of income in 20 or 30 years instead of 100 years.

A third method for limiting hoarding would be to establish wage and price controls. A wage and price freeze stops wages and prices from rising, at least for a while. Two problems with this method are: 1) wages and prices tend to rise rapidly when the freeze is lifted, and 2) the level where wages and prices are frozen may not be fair. Some wages may be too high and others too low. Freezing them does no good.

The fourth and worst method for limiting hoarding is through a progressive income tax. A progressive income tax taxes higher incomes at a higher percentage than lower incomes. This method has two major problems. First, a higher percentage can still leave some people with much larger incomes than other people. For example, a 50 percent tax on a million dollars leaves the taxpayer with $500,000. A 10 percent tax on $10,000 leaves the taxpayer with $9,000. The end result is not noticeably fairer than before taxes.

The second problem with a progressive income tax method of limiting hoarding is tax loopholes. People with large incomes quickly use their money to influence the government to pass exemptions so that they can avoid taxes. The tax law may say that they must pay 50 percent but, with all the loopholes, large incomes may not be taxed at all.

The results we can expect from practicing Lifetime Economics are:

1. More Wealth and Health,
2. Less Work, and
3. More Free Time.

In short, Lifetime Economics would result in more time to enjoy life.

Chapter 26

The Politics of Remodeling

The nice thing about using GDP per hour of work as the nation's wage and price standard is that it does not require a law or constitutional amendment to be implemented. It requires only a simple arithmetic calculation on easily available data. This means that any group can begin to implement the standard by bringing it into their wage and salary negotiations. Of course, government sanction would make implementation easier and more certain. If each year the government announced the standard as official, it would encourage its use. Applying the measure yourself immediately is far easier than having to pass a law or Constitutional Amendment.

If everyone who would benefit from its implementation would support it, implementation would come quickly. Everyone would benefit. The benefit is most clear for people who are now paid very little. Their wages would rise substantially. All the merchants who sell goods and services that these people need would also benefit as higher wages meant more purchasing power in the hands of people in need.

People who already receive the standard wage would also benefit but less obviously. They could expect their taxes to go down because less would be needed for welfare payments. They could expect their city streets to be safer as secure employment goes up and crime goes down. And they could expect the quality of what they buy to rise as people focus on making higher quality products.

The people who would be hardest to convince to support lifetime economics would be those who now receive incomes in the hundreds of thousands and millions of dollars. Most of the money they receive is useless to them. They cannot eat enough, wear enough, or travel enough to spend millions of dollars in a year. Most of the money in excess of reasonable living expenses is of no real value to them. They may not see it that way. Imagine telling the Pharaohs of Egypt that the pyramids would not get them to heaven. However, the new model has to be sold on its merits to them and everyone else.

When automobiles were invented, everyone who made horse drawn carriages and harness equipment, bred horses, or owned carriages saw automobiles as a threat. People invested in the present short-time economic system may see lifetime economics as a threat. People who obtain money without working may find things wrong with a system that expects them to work, albeit an ever-shrinking amount of work.

Orthodox economists may object to lifetime economics because it is like a foreign language to them, a cultural crisis. I see economics, as we know it today, as beyond repair. We have tried to compete and hoard as supply and demand economics requires, and luxury has gone to the few while the many hunger and thirst.

It is easy to understand why people who benefit from the existing system and who are intellectually heavily invested in it would oppose the new model. It is more difficult to understand why people who would gain from the new model would oppose it, but some will. People do not necessarily do what is in their own best interests. The lottery is an example. Far more than 99 percent of the people who play the lottery lose; it is not in their interest to play. Yet they play because they hope to be the rare exception and win. It is foolish to gamble against such odds. It is more foolish to gamble with our lives. We can work together and all be wealthy. We cannot repair the present system. We must remodel. Will you help? Is the most wealth for the least work worth it?

What must be done?

1. Move toward a wage and price standard of GDP/Total Hours Worked,
2. Convert from interest as a rate to a bookkeeping fee,
3. Reduce the workweek by the rate of unemployment, and
4. Have government create money as needed interest and debt free.

Chapter 27

Cooperation: The Wealth of Nations Game

Words are easy, not easy in the sense of spelling, grammar, and such, but easy in the sense that you can say just about anything you want with words. You can lie; you can fantasize; you can speculate. That's what makes movies and science fiction such fun. But our business here is about real life. How can we know that anything I have written here, or anything you can read in textbooks, really works as advertised and is good policy? Simulation is our best option for testing ideas.

We have many examples of the use of simulation. Soldiers practice war with war games. Airlines train pilots in simulators, devices with all the features of a cockpit, where pilots can practice every kind of situation before they actually get into a real plane. The shape of the modern jet aircraft fuselage was achieved by using wind tunnels where air turbulence could be watched and the design adjusted to minimize it. Wind tunnels were used to improve airflow over automobile bodies as well.

Cooperation: The Wealth of Nations Game is an economics simulation. It is both a board game and a computer game. The board version consists of different land types, grassland, forest, lakes, desert, and mountains. Players place cities on the board with the goal of obtained resources that meet five needs of the people in their cities: food, fiber, wood, metal, and fuel. They obtain the resources by having their people produce them and/or by trading with other players. To trade resources, players must employ some of their people in building transportation. They also have the option of educating people in their cities to higher skill levels to improve their effectiveness and efficiency.

As a simulation, Cooperation: The Wealth of Nations Game enables players to play by different rules to see the consequences of the differences. The first game is Barter: the beginners' game. The second game is Majority Rule: the socialist game. The third game is Making Money: the capitalist game. Playing these three games over many years with my sociology students produced Autonomy: the expert tournament game. Autonomy combines the best features of the other three games and avoids their weaknesses. It simulates how to achieve the most wealth with the least work!

The popular board game Monopoly started out as a simulation of Henry George's ideas published in 1879 in his book, *Progress and Poverty*. Lizzie Magie invented the game so that people could understand Henry George's ideas without having to read a book of more than 500 pages. She called her game The Landlord's Game. She applied for a patent on her game in 1903. It had two parts. The first part showed the destructive nature of income without work, which Henry George called rent. The second part of Lizzie Magie's game showed George's solution, which was a tax on rent.

When Parker Brothers got the game from Charles Darrow in 1935, they dropped the second part. Monopoly as we know it is just the destructive part. Only one person wins and that is achieved by bankrupting everyone else, not a very good model for real life. You can read about it on the Internet at:
http://www.adena.com/adena/mo/index.htm

With that in mind, Bob Gill and I invented Cooperation: The Wealth of Nations Games. We did not want people to think it was just a game. We wanted players to understand that they were simulating different economic systems. Students helped develop the game starting in 1975. In the years since then, the game has been improved. A few years ago, students in computer science programmed the game to play on a computer. We continue to develop the game today. You can download it for free from http://hourmoney.org. From there you can contact me, Bob Blain, for more information, including how to obtain the board game. The file is about 2.5MB and you will need an unzipping program like Winzip.

Autonomy is called the expert tournament game because it shows how an economy based on hour money would enable everyone to be wealthy with a minimum of work. I invite you to get Cooperation: The Wealth of Nations Game and experience for yourself the advantages and disadvantages of barter, socialism, and capitalism, and the way Autonomy can benefit us all with the most wealth for the least work.

Chapter 28
Sovereignty

The basic idea I have tried to support in this book is that we can achieve our destiny of the most wealth for the least work by sharing the work and sharing the wealth. Sharing the work minimizes the work each person must do and optimizes the wealth produced. Our problem is entropy. Everything wears out. The general direction of energy flow is downhill. The sun is our main source of energy. As Bucky Fuller liked to point out, the sun's energy is our current income. Fossil fuels, stored sun's energy, he would remind us, are our savings accounts. He recommended that we use our current income rather than our savings accounts.

Our job is to build things back up. We build our bodies back up when we eat. We build our minds back up with lifelong learning. We build our structures back up through proper maintenance, repair, remodeling, and replacement. In building things back up, we use energy, which is to say, we produce entropy. Our challenge is to work effectively and efficiently. We do that by cooperating. To cooperate, we must communicate, specialize, and reciprocate. Language, writing, numbers and money facilitate those processes.

Money is the big problem obstructing our progress toward the most wealth for the least work because the money unit is undefined. By defining it, we can bring clarity to the degree to which we are sharing the work and sharing the wealth. I am following the recommendation of others and the evidence in advocating that we adopt an hour of work as the world money unit.

Just as the units of the Metric System make measurement easy and amicable, an hour of work can show us where we are economically and sociologically. By converting all incomes and prices into their work time equivalents, we can begin the process of sharing the work and the wealth more equitably. We can judge incomes, prices, and money exchange rates more wisely from their center of gravity, Gross Domestic Product divided by Total Hours Worked. With that center clearly in view, we can begin to adjust toward that center of gravity.

Inequalities could continue to exist, but we would want them to be justified on any number of possible grounds, for example, investment, risk, hardship, and intensity. We would want to correct any inequities, cases where equal work is compensated, for no good reason, with unequal pay. Most of all, we should want to eliminate iniquities, for example, thefts and hoarding.

I am reminded of a sentence that appeared in a letter to the editor opposing the adoption of Alexander Hamilton's plan in 1790 to fund the economy of the new United States with borrowed money. "The pen of history will detect and expose the folly of the arguments in favor of the proposed system, as well as the iniquity." The word was iniquity, not inequity.

The Congressman from Georgia, James Jackson, speaking in the First Congress on February 9, 1790, warned, "Let us take warning by the errors of Europe and guard against the adoption of a system followed by calamities so general. Though our present debt be but a few millions, in the course of a single century, it may be multiplied to an extent we dare not think of."

The iniquity was that many members of that Congress had purchased the debt certificates from holders who thought the certificates would soon be worthless, themselves knowing that they were about to pass a law to pay interest on those certificates at their face value for many years to come. As James Callender put it at the time in the *Philadelphia Gazette*, legislators passed the Funding Act with "the single view of enriching themselves."

That funding system is still in place, and debt has indeed multiplied to an extent we dare not think of.

As I explained earlier, Sovereignty is the name of an organization founded in 1989 by Ken Bohnsack of Freeport, Illinois; its purpose is to have Congress fund public capital projects, such as schools, roads, bridges, water supply and treatment plants and repairs with loans from the federal government interest free. Interest is the factor that mathematically causes debt to grow exponentially, as I explained earlier. Bohnsack's idea means that tax-supported bodies like city, county, and state governments and school boards would pay only the costs of construction and repair, saving taxpayers billions of dollars that would otherwise go to pay interest.

Bohnsack and others have succeeded in getting close to 4,000 tax-supported bodies to formally vote to support the plan. Bohnsack calls his organization Sovereignty to keep in mind that a government that borrows money gives up some of its sovereignty to its creditors. By having the federal government supply tax bodies with loans of government-created money, the federal government would recover its sovereignty. You can contact Ken Bohnsack through his web site listed in the Acknowledgement statement at the beginning of this book.

In conclusion, I cannot say that everything in this book is absolutely correct. Like any remodeling job, the ideas in this book are meant to paint a picture of the new house. In the actual process of construction we may find that we need to make some adjustments. The overall plan for the new house, however, is to have a place where we can fulfill the destiny toward which all of human cultural history is aimed, a world of human beings living well, as happily as Mother Earth makes possible.

Let me close with a few words from Ralph Waldo Emerson (1803-1882):

It is for man to tame the chaos; on every side, whilst he lives, to scatter the seeds of science and of song, that climate, corn, animals, men, may be milder, and the germs of love and benefit may be multiplied.3

Love would put a new face on this weary world...One day all men will be lovers; and every calamity will be dissolved in the universal sunshine.4

Virtue is the business of the universe.

Amen.

---

3 Ralph Waldo Emerson, *Essays and Lectures.* The Library of America, 1983:632.
4 *The Complete Works of Ralph Waldo Emerson.* New York: Wm. H. Wise:78-79.

Bob Blain's Related Publications

1985 The information chain theory of cooperation, *International Journal of Comparative Sociology* 26, March-June: 75-89.

1987 United States Public and Private Debt: 1791-2000, *International Social Science Journal* 114, November: 577-591.

1996 Defining exchange rate parity in terms of GDP per hour of work. *Applied Behavioral Science Review.* Vol. 4, Number 1, 55-79.

2002 The hour is the *de facto* world money unit. In: Mieczyslaw Dobija (Ed.) *Monetary Unit Stability in Holistic Approach.* Leon Kozminski Academy, Warsaw, Poland. 27-53.

Conference Presentations

1979 "Making money a more accurate measure of value," Eastern Economics Association, Boston.

1987 "Improving life expectancy by enlarging the scale of cooperation," Midwest Sociological Society, Chicago.

1993 "Income equality and national wealth," Illinois Sociological Association, Rockford, Illinois.

1994 "Causes of national wealth," Midwest Sociological Society, St. Louis.

1994 "The role of exchange rates and the International Monetary Fund in the maintenance of First World hegemony," Midwest Sociological Society, St. Louis.

2002 "The hour is the *de facto* world money unit." International Workshop on Monetary Stability in Holistic Approach: Leon Kozminski Academy, Warsaw, Poland.

Other

1981 Cooperation: The Wealth of Nations Game – an economics simulation board game.

1986 to present - Board member of Sovereignty, whose goal is to fund public facilities with U.S. Treasury money interest-free.

1991 Toured New Zealand for a month at the invitation of the Democratic Party of New Zealand to explain Sovereignty to government, newspapers, and radio audiences.

Current Priority

Promoting an hour of work as the world base money unit.

About the Author

Internationally published author and professor, Bob Blain, received his Masters degree in sociology from Harvard University and his Doctor of Philosophy from the University of Massachusetts. He taught sociology at Ohio State University and retired from Southern Illinois University Edwardsville in 2001 after 35 years of teaching and research. Bob sees himself as re-tired in the sense of having new treads. He is joyfully committed to promoting adoption of an hour of work as the world's base money unit and is happy to be able to offer you the computer game he invented with his friend, Bob Gill, Cooperation: the Wealth of Nations Game, which simulates how Hour Money would lead us to the most wealth with the least work.

Printed in the United States
119368LV00004B/199-222/A